THE WORLD CUP

HEROES, HOODLUMS, HIGH-KICKS and HEAD-BUTTS

PAUL HANSFORD

hardie grant books

MELBOURNE · LONDON

Published in 2014 by Hardie Grant Books

Hardie Grant Books (Australia)
Ground Floor, Building 1
658 Church Street
Richmond, Victoria 3121
www.hardiegrant.com.au

Hardie Grant Books (UK)
Dudley House, North Suite
34–35 Southampton Street
London WC2E 7HF
www.hardiegrant.co.uk

Cataloguing-in-publication data available from the catalogue
of the National Library of Australia at www.nla.gov.au

The World Cup: Heroes, Hoodlums,
High-Kicks and Head-Butts
ISBN 978 1 74270 743 3

Cover designer Josh Durham/Design by Committee
Text design and typesetting Pauline Haas
Typeset in Bauer Bodini
Printed and bound in Australia by Griffin Press

For my 'dynamic duo', Lukas and Kasper.

Contents

INTRODUCTION

66 Win or die! 99 — *Benito Mussolini, 1938*

66 Both are very hard to stay without [but] I'm sure
sex wouldn't be so rewarding as this World Cup.
It's not that sex isn't good but the World Cup is every
four years and sex is not. 99 — *Ronaldo, 2002*

It's not worth wasting your breath debating it — the FIFA World
Cup is the greatest sporting event in the world. Every four years
more than 200 countries fight it out for just thirty-one places
(the hosts get a free pass, having bought all the food and booze)
in the richest, most prestigious and keenly fought tournament
on the planet.

Billions of football fans put their regular lives on pause for
the month-long football fest, including an estimated 715 million
who watched the final in 2006 and more than 3 million spectators
who went through the turnstiles in 2010. (It seems FIFA are still
counting viewers from the last final, as many fell into a deep
state of shock after being traumatised by the Netherlands' 'kick
anything with a pulse' tactics.) To belabour the point just a little
longer, in South Africa 390,000 hot dogs and three-quarters of
a million litres of beer were sold in the stadiums — admittedly
a bit of a disappointing figure, but my mate Andy and I had to
return home after the knockout stages ...

The World Cup's rivals don't measure up in comparison.
The Super Bowl is too American, Wimbledon is too white (clothing
and participants), the World Series isn't a *world* series and the
Tour de France is a bit too 'dopey'. Of course, there is the elephant
in the room — the Olympics — but when you consider that the

only Olympic events that come close to matching the viewing figures of the World Cup (the opening and closing ceremonies) are not even sport, then there's no need to even go into whether twirling a ribbon on a stick or walking really fast are actual sports.

Having covered three tournaments in my time working for *Shoot!* and *Australian FourFourTwo*, I have been fortunate enough to witness in person the drama, passion, hatred, violence and farce that is the World Cup finals.

Some of the most memorable moments of my time spent in France, Germany and South Africa include having bottles thrown at me by rioting England fans in Marseille, chasing a German kid who'd stolen my bag through a train station at 3 am after I'd nodded off on a bench, and witnessing a fellow journalist sleep through a World Cup Final in the press box because he'd had a bit too much champagne in celebration of getting a ticket.

And that's even before getting to the football: Michael Owen's goal against Argentina in 1998, Lilian Thuram's second against Croatia in the semifinal of the same year, Tim Cahill's heroics in Australia's stunning come-from-behind win against Japan in 2006 and watching Ronaldo score, Beckham hit a free kick, Zidane pass, Iniesta move ...

My memories of watching the World Cup on TV as a youngster are just as vivid: the short shorts and big hair of '82, the spider-like shadow on the pitch of the Estadio Azteca in '86, the tears of Gazza and *Nessun Dorma* in Italia 90 and the humiliation of the missed penalty in USA 94 (Diana Ross, not Roberto Baggio). I can recall the exploits of Zico, Maradona, Socrates, Rossi and Lineker as if I were still the wide-eyed, ginger-haired kid who stayed up to all hours to watch every game of every tournament (even if I didn't know where Honduras was and couldn't pronounce 'Goikoetxea' properly).

The reasons the World Cup stands as the ultimate sporting event are innumerable, but for me the allure of the World Cup is the memories it evokes. Of course, there are the football ones —

the great games, players and goals — but more important are the personal ones it creates: watching England games with my dad; recreating Paolo Rossi's goals with my brother in the back garden (he was always the crestfallen Brazilian goalkeeper); and the lesson I was taught as a nine-year-old when Harald Schumacher's assault on Patrick Battiston went unpunished, letting me know in no uncertain terms that the good guys don't always win.

So I'd like to think of *The World Cup: Heroes, hoodlums, high-kicks and head-butts* as a stroll down football's memory lane, shining a light on the great World Cup tournaments from not just the modern era, but from the eras of our fathers and our fathers' fathers. Along the way you will be introduced to the legendary players, the greatest games, the biggest shocks and a whole host of weird and wonderful tales that help create the World Cup's storied history.

Enjoy.

A BRIEF HISTORY OF THE FIFA WORLD CUP FINALS

The dominant themes in FIFA's formation of a World Cup tournament at the turn of the last century are very similar to the governing body's main motivations moving into the 21st century and beyond: to control the world game and make shedloads of money.

At the turn of the 20th century, a struggle was taking place in football's corridors of power. The English Football Association (FA) ruled the roost; as the 'founding fathers' of the game, they were the sport's key influencers, principally through the organising of football's jewel in the crown, the Olympic tournament.

However, across Europe there was a growing feeling that a global governing body was needed. European associations were placing pressure on the FA to become more involved in the international side of the game; but, having 'invented' football, the English saw the game as their ball — and they were not going to let anyone else play with it.

Led by French journalist Robert Guérin and lawyer-turned-administrator Jules Rimet, the 'breakaway' associations believed the FA's position was untenable in the long run and began work on the formation of a world body. Recognising the importance of involving the FA, Guérin approached them to become involved, but, not for the last time, the FA maintained an isolationist position — with a heavy serving of arrogance on the side — and told 'Johnny foreigner' to leave their game alone, responding that they 'couldn't see the advantage' of the proposal.

Not put off by a few snooty Brits, on 21 May 1904 representatives from the football associations of France, Belgium, Denmark, Switzerland, the Netherlands, Sweden and Spain gathered to agree on the formation of the Fédération Internationale de Football Association (FIFA) and installed Guérin as its first president. In a two-fingered salute to the FA (which actually gave its blessing to FIFA's formation and joined a year later), the most significant statute agreed upon that day was as follows: 'The international Federation is the only organisation with the right to organise an international competition.' England's ball had been kicked over the fence and the Europeans weren't about to give it back …

A sixteen-team tournament was agreed upon the following year and scheduled to take place alongside the 1906 FIFA Congress in Switzerland, but a lack of time and financial commitment from potential competitors meant the first World Cup had to be canned for the foreseeable future.

FIFA took over the organisation of Olympic football in 1912, but what was once the world's most popular tournament was becoming a shadow of its former self due to the growth of the professional game. The problems extended as far back as 1908, when the Games had only four participants due to fixture clashes with domestic leagues and the ineligibility of professional players. Post WWI, the tournament was beset by rumours of 'shamateurism' — professional players taking part on the quiet — and FIFA, now led by Rimet, realised the only solution was a world championship tournament for professional footballers. In 1926, Rimet's right-hand man, fellow Frenchman Henri Delauney, summed up FIFA's attitude when he said:

"Today international football can no longer be held within the confines of the Olympics; and many countries where professionalism is now recognised and organised cannot any longer be represented there by their best players."

With vast sums of money to be made from an official world championship, Rimet moved to separate FIFA's proposed 'World Cup' from the Olympic tournament, so as to avoid any conflicts over professional participants. In May 1928, at the FIFA congress in Amsterdam, the World Cup finals was agreed upon and, at the following year's congress in Barcelona, despite interest from Italy, the Netherlands, Spain and Sweden, Uruguay was confirmed as the first host. While much was made of the Uruguayan government's decision to cover the costs of the entire tournament, a far more significant decision flew under the radar: FIFA decided it would take 10 per cent of the World Cup's gross income for itself.

And with that, the World Cup, the greatest sporting event in the world — and FIFA's cash cow — was born.

Uruguay 1930

Celebrating the centenary of its independence and boasting the stunning (but unfinished) Estadio Centenario as its centrepiece, Uruguay seemed like the perfect host for the first World Cup. However, appearances can be deceiving. Despite having secured nine nations from the Americas to compete, with just two months from kick-off there were no confirmed European participants.

This was in part due to the long travel times and the effects of the Wall Street Crash, and in part, 'We're not coming because you didn't pick us to host the thing'; the Netherlands, Hungary, Italy, Spain and Sweden all threw their toys out of the pram and refused to travel after being overlooked. (None of the British sides attended either, after pulling out of FIFA in 1928 over an argument about amateurism.) But, in the same manner they would overcome future host nations' 'problems' — such as unfinished stadiums, inadequate infrastructure and intolerance to minority groups — FIFA weren't going to let the small matter of no teams spoil their party. Second-tier nations France, Belgium, Yugoslavia and Romania — funded, selected and coached by their ruler, King Carol, no less — were drafted in and they joined various FIFA officials and bigwigs on the *SS Conte Verde* for the two-week journey across the Atlantic, picking up the Brazil team along the way. (Unfortunately, the results of a keenly contested 'Shuffleboard World Cup' on board seem to be lost to history ...)

On the pitch, the host nation — and double Olympic champion — was tipped for victory, with Argentina and France also favoured. The first two World Cup games took place simultaneously on 13 July 1930, with France beating Mexico 4–1 — Frenchman Lucien Laurent scoring the first-ever World Cup goal on nineteen minutes — and the USA besting Belgium 3–0. With the two South American nations seemingly on a collision course, Argentina faced the USA and Uruguay played Yugoslavia in the semifinals, and 6–1 victories for both sides set up a highly anticipated final.

An estimated 300,000 Argentineans made their way across the River Plate to Montevideo for the big day on 30 July, but it was to be the hosts who emerged victorious, 4–2, thanks to second-half goals from Pedro Cea, Santos Iriarte and the one-handed Hector Castro (he lost his hand in a childhood accident, not during the game). The historic victory by *La Celeste* sparked parties across the country and the stoning of the Uruguayan consulate in Buenos Aires. It would seem the significance of the first World Cup was not lost on anyone involved.

Italy 1934

The 1934 finals in Italy highlighted the burgeoning popularity of the competition; it was the first World Cup to be broadcast live on the radio, and a qualifying tournament was needed to whittle down the thirty-two applicants to sixteen participants. It also shone a light on how the World Cup was already being used by FIFA for financial gain, and by shady politicians eager to legitimise their regimes by association. Why else would

FIFA award Benito Mussolini — a leader who had outlawed all political parties and was torturing and killing his own citizens — the finals?

One team did not take part, in protest: the champions, Uruguay. Not for political reasons, however, but as payback for the Italians boycotting their 1930 tournament. South American 'brothers' Argentina and Brazil both sent under-strength teams in (semi) protest too.

All this didn't seem to bother the organisers, who had enough on their plate planning a tournament across eight cities and keeping the ever-increasing interference of Mussolini in check. (Jules Rimet was said to have remarked that Mussolini was acting more like the president of FIFA than Rimet was.) The long arm of Il Duce was always lurking in the background during the 1934 finals, especially in his supposed selection of 'Italy-friendly' referees.

One rule change that proved disastrous for the tournament was the move to a straight knockout format; Romania, Belgium, France, the Netherlands, Egypt, the USA, Brazil and Argentina all went home after just one match, denying fans the opportunity to see many of the world's best players for an extended period.

Led by legendary coach Vittorio Pozzo, Italy were strong favourites for the title, especially after selecting several *oriundi* — Argentinean players of Italian descent — including Luis Monti, who had played a huge role helping the *albiceleste* make the World Cup Final four years earlier. Their nearest challengers appeared to be the Austrian 'Wunderteam', led by the hugely talented Matthias 'The Paper Man' Sindelar, and a highly regarded Czechoslovakian side featuring strikers Antonin Puc and Oldřich Nejedlý.

After a first round of games that followed the formbook, Germany, Austria and Czechoslovakia progressed to the semis thanks to wins over Sweden, Hungary and Switzerland respectively. Italy, however, were taken to a replay by a stubborn Spain, and only booked their place in the final four twenty-four hours later, thanks to a Giuseppe Meazza header (and a Swiss referee so obviously on Mussolini's payroll that he might as well have worn calf-high leather boots and goosestepped around the pitch for ninety minutes).

Just two days later Italy faced mighty Austria, and a solitary first-half goal from Argentina-born winger Enrique Guaita and another friendly ref helped decide the game. Czechoslovakia had a much smoother passage to the finals, as the mercurial Nejedlý scored a hat-trick against the hapless Germans.

Played against a backdrop that was, according to one historian, more fascist rally than World Cup game, the final was a tight affair, pitting the pass-and-move philosophy of Czechoslovakia against the tight defence and pacey counter-attack of Italy. Puc stunned the home crowd by scoring with just fourteen minutes left, and if František Svoboda's shot had squeezed in rather than hitting the post, the game would've been beyond Italy.

But, possibly spurred on by Mussolini's 'win or die' telegram that was read to them before the match, Italy wouldn't give up — and a stunning shot by Raimundo Orsi with eight minutes to go levelled the tie. The *Azzurri* were in the ascendancy, and an Angelo Schiavio strike five minutes into extra time was all that was needed to win Italy the World Cup — and maybe save the team and coaches from the wrath of an angry dictator.

France 1938

The dark clouds of war were forming over Europe, but a little bit of fascism wasn't going to stop the mighty FIFA from holding their showcase event. National socialism cast a long shadow over the finals in France from the outset, with Hitler's annexation of Austria leading to the selection of a 'Greater Germany' team featuring more than half a dozen Austrians. (So much for the superiority of the German nation, eh?)

Mussolini was up to his old tricks too, getting involved in team selection and ordering the team to play a game in 'fascist' black, while both Germany and Italy gave Nazi salutes before their matches. Anti-fascist protests, especially from exiled Italians living in France, took place both inside and outside the grounds (the saluting Germans were pelted with bottles from the crowd), leading to ugly scenes all over the country.

From a football perspective, the '38 finals featured the first legendary team — Italy — and the first bona fide superstar, Brazil's Leônidas. Italy joined the pantheon of greats by virtue of a second consecutive title, their team featuring the irresistible talents of Giuseppe Meazza, Pietro Rava and goal-getter supreme Silvio Piola. Brazil's Leônidas — aka 'The Black Diamond' or 'The Rubber Man' — took the tournament by storm; he was the finals' top goalscorer and made his name with a hat-trick in the brilliant 6–5 win over Poland. Brazil coach Adhemar Pimenta's decision to rest him for the semifinal against Italy (a game they lost) is still one of the most controversial decisions the finals has ever seen.

The knockout group stages saw favourites Italy, Brazil and Hungary progress but it also threw up a couple of shockers, with Germany losing to Switzerland and Cuba seeing off Romania (although they were duly spanked 8–0 by Sweden in the next round). The most notable game in the quarterfinals was Italy's victory over France, ensuring that for the first time the host nation would not win the world title. In the semifinals, Italy beat a Leônidas-less Brazil 2–1 in Marseille, and Hungary swept Sweden aside 5–1, thanks to Gyula Zsengellér's hat-trick.

In the final, high-scoring Hungary were no match for the polished Italy, with Giuseppe Meazza giving a masterclass in attacking football. Goals from Titkos and Sárosi kept Hungary in it, but Silvio Piola scored twice in the 4–2 win that saw Italy — and their coach, Vittorio Pozzo — crowned as all-time greats.

Brazil 1950

After the darkness of the war years, the World Cup needed a boost. Granting Brazil the rights to stage the 1950 finals was a step in the right direction — the mighty 200,000 capacity Maracanã Stadium built for the event was a testament to their football-mad credentials — and when 'mighty' England were confirmed as participants for the first time, things were looking up. Even the World Cup trophy was given a reboot, newly named the Jules Rimet Trophy.

But we are talking about international football here and, as kick-off approached, the tournament soon reverted to type, becoming blighted by more early withdrawals than a behind-the-bike-sheds session at a Catholic school prom night. The absence of the Eastern European nations was understandable due to the ravages of the war, but Argentina, France and Scotland's last-minute pull-outs were less excusable. (Argentina left due to a dispute with the Brazilian Federation, Scotland wouldn't accept a place after finishing second in their qualifying group, while the French didn't like how much they had to travel.) The organisers were put in the awkward position of only having thirteen teams, and the odd number of sides played havoc with the groupings. To make matters worse, FIFA decided the 1950 tournament would not have a traditional final but a final round-robin group stage (four teams in what was dramatically called the 'Final Pool') to crown the world champions.

The strangeness continued on the pitch. It began with England's earth-shattering 1–0 loss to the USA, a defeat so unbelievable that the British newspapers thought it was a typo on the news wire and changed the scoreline to 10–0 in favour of the Three Lions. A subsequent 1–0 defeat to Spain sent England's superstars home with their heads in their hands. The holders, Italy, were knocked out by Sweden (although Italy were a shadow of their former selves after the tragic Superga air disaster the year before) and Brazil needed a final group game win over Yugoslavia to ensure they advanced. The finals descended into farce with Pool 4, a group consisting of just Uruguay and Bolivia (after France's withdrawal); the victorious *Celeste* progressed to the final group having played only one match.

Brazil really found their form in the final group stage — thanks to the attacking flair of Zizinho, Ademir and Jair — as they racked up a 7–1 spanking of Sweden and a 6–1 victory over Spain. Uruguay kept pace, although their draw against Spain meant that Brazil only needed to draw against their South American neighbours to win the World Cup in the final game.

Unofficial estimates had the crowd at 200,000 for the 'final' on 16 July, a day that still lives on in infamy across Brazil. The entire nation expected nothing less than victory, and it looked to be theirs after Friaça scored early in the second half. But Juan Schiaffino levelled in the 66th minute and then, with eleven minutes remaining, winger Alcides Ghiggia broke down the right wing and hit a shot that took keeper Moacir Barbosa by surprise at his near post. The goal silenced the entire stadium in a second, destroyed the life of the Brazil keeper and created a shockwave that still reverberates through the Brazilian psyche even today.

Switzerland 1954

When the World Cup finally returned to Europe in 1954, Switzerland was the obvious choice to host. Untouched by the devastation suffered by the rest of the continent during the war, and the home of governing body, FIFA, the Swiss were able to invest in new stadiums in six venues across the country, including the wonderfully named Wankdorf Stadium in Bern.

Ensuring the nets were securely attached to the posts proved to be one of the most important tasks, as it turned out to be one of the highest-scoring finals on record. A hundred and forty goals flew in at an average of five per game, with the rampant Hungary singlehandedly responsible for twenty-seven of them.

In fact, there had never been a more clear-cut favourite for the World Cup than Hungary in 1954. Led by the 'Galloping Major', Ferenc Puskás, the 'Magical Magyars' came into the tournament off the back of a four-year undefeated streak, including a 6–3 footballing education handed out to England at Wembley in November 1953. Playing one of the first versions of a 4–2–4 formation, Hungary were a dream to watch and backed up their credentials by beating North Korea 9–0 and Germany 8–3 in their first two group games.

FIFA tinkered with the finals format yet again, this time having groups with two seeded teams playing two non-seeded teams, but not each other. This saw the usual suspects advance relatively unscathed to the next stage, which was probably for the best, considering the fireworks that followed. Firstly, England's World Cup disappointment continued, as they were knocked out in the quarters by Uruguay. A knocking-out of a different kind took place when Brazil and Hungary met; two of the most gifted teams in the game resorted to kicking, punching, gouging and bottle-smashing in what became known as 'The Battle of Bern' (see Chapter 8 for more details). Oh yeah, Hungary won 4–2. Meanwhile, the Germans — playing in their first World Cup since WWII — worked to a strict … ahem … battle plan to make the final, fielding a weakened team in the 8–3 loss to Hungary so they could avoid Brazil in the next round. It paid off, and wins over Yugoslavia and Austria saw them progress to the final to face Hungary, 4–2 winners over Uruguay.

The final was a huge mismatch on paper: unseeded Germany against invincible Hungary. And the match looked to be over as a contest after only eight minutes, thanks to goals from Puskás and Czibor, but Germany hadn't read the script, and by the twenty-minute mark the teams were on level terms. Spurred on by inspirational captain Fritz Walter — and aided by new screw-in studs on their boots for the wet conditions — Germany weathered the second-half storm, Hungary twice hitting the woodwork and having a shot cleared off the line. Helmut Rahn struck a shot into the far corner to stun the Magyars in the 84th minute, and a controversially disallowed Puskás goal at the death confirmed Germany as surprise world champions.

The match became known as 'The Miracle of Bern' and changed the footballing destinies of the two nations: Germany became a World Cup 'uberteam' to be written off at their opponents' peril, while Hungary disappeared as a world power after the 1956 Revolution saw the break-up of their wonderful squad.

Sweden 1958

The 1958 World Cup will always be remembered as the finals that introduced the incomparable Pelé to the world. Seventeen-year-old Edson Arantes do Nascimento inspired a team playing a unique brand of football — dubbed *jogo bonito*, the 'beautiful game' — to its first World Cup title and ushered in a new footballing powerhouse. Echoing the 4–2–4 formation of Hungary in the mid-'50s, Brazil's combination of pace, skill and trickery made the game look easy at times — but that belied a newfound tactical awareness and hard work ethic (the team had a three-month 'boot camp' and toured Europe extensively before arriving in Sweden). It also helped that they had the most feared attacking frontline in all of football: Pelé and Vavá up front, flanked by Mário Zagallo and Garrincha.

But it wasn't all smooth sailing for the samba boys. Although Pelé and Garrincha would emerge as the tournament's brightest stars, they didn't feature in the Brazil team until the third game of the group stages, and only then at the behest of teammates who could see the team needed an extra spark. Pelé's exclusion was due in part to injury — one so severe that his selection to the squad looked in jeopardy — and his age; the Brazil coaches knew they had something special but were concerned about a seventeen-year-old being able to handle grown men aiming their boots at his shins for an entire tournament. Garrincha, in contrast, was seen as a wildcard: a mercurial, free-spirited talent whose artistry was impossible to overlook as the tournament progressed.

With traditional powerhouses Italy and Uruguay failing to qualify, the 1958 finals marked the only time all four British nations competed but, in a reversal of form and expectation, Northern Ireland and Wales advanced from the group stages, while Scotland and England were home before the postcards. Other favourites included hosts Sweden, coached by Brit George Raynor and finally able to call on a fully professional team, and the free-scoring France, led by '*Le Tandem Terrible*' of Raymond Kopa and Just Fontaine. A last-minute replacement for the injured René Bliard, Fontaine scored thirteen goals in six games, a finals record that still stands today.

The tournament proper didn't really kick off until the quarters, with Pelé's first World Cup goal seeing off a stubborn Wales, and France smashing Northern Ireland 4–0. West Germany and Sweden joined them in the semis, after beating Yugoslavia and the Soviet Union respectively. Buoyed by a noisy home crowd, the first semifinal saw Sweden take care of West Germany 3–1, thanks to two goals in the final ten minutes. Brazil and France played out a tight affair in the other semi, until France's Robert Jonquet broke his leg in the second half (with no substitutes in those days, Jonquet hopped about on the wing shouting, 'It's only a flesh wound,' for the rest of the game) and Pelé went goal crazy, scoring a hat-trick in just twenty-three minutes to seal a 5–2 win.

In the final, Sweden proved no match for a rampant Brazil and, despite taking the lead through Nils Liedholm, could not stop the South American juggernaut's date with destiny. Thanks to two goals apiece from Vavá and Pelé, the South Americans became the first nation to win the World Cup outside their home continent.

Chile 1962

Struck by a devastating earthquake two years previous, Chile was a doubt to host the finals until their FA president, Carlos Dittborn, made a heartfelt plea to FIFA: 'It is because we now have nothing that we must have the World Cup.' In possibly the only time the FIFA bigwigs let their hearts rule rather than their wallets, the tournament remained in Chile, only for it to be hit by a natural phenomenon of a different kind in the form of Brazil's Garrincha.

The man known as 'The Little Bird' took the 1962 finals by storm and was the inspiration behind Brazil's second world title, creating and scoring goals with an impact only Maradona in 1986 has ever matched. Quite where he got his energy from is a mystery, as the twenty-five-year-old was well known for liking the ladies and liquor. (He was also a father of seven, although not all were conceived during the '62 tournament.)

Other than the exploits of the mercurial Brazilian, the Chilean tournament was quite a dour affair. A new rule change stating that goal average would decide which team would progress if there was a tie at the end of the group stages led to more defensive — and rougher — tactics. A new 'angrier' World Cup reached boiling point at what is known as 'The Battle of Santiago', a brutal ninety minutes between Italy and Chile that featured fisticuffs, a neck-high kick, one broken nose and a couple of red cards (see Chapter 8 for more details). Many of the matches were also poorly attended (the fans were obviously unaware they might get to see some decent biff), especially outside the capital, where a measly 7000 turned up to see England play Bulgaria.

When teams did decide to play some football, there were a couple of gems, most notably Colombia's brilliant comeback against the Soviet Union, transforming a 3–0 deficit into a 4–4 draw. Spain and Brazil also played a peach of a group game at the Estadio Sausalito, where two late, late goals from 'The White Pelé', Amarildo, saw Spain — and Ferenc Puskás, now exiled

from Hungary and wearing the red of his adopted country —
crash out 2–1.

Brazil took care of England 3–1 in the quarters, and Chile
4–2 in the semis, although the game against the hosts was not
without intrigue. Garrincha was sent off for an innocuous foul,
and by rights should have been suspended for the final. However,
after much lobbying he was allowed to play in the final against
Czechoslovakia.

Brazil were heavy favourites in the final, but Czechoslovakia
boasted Viliam Schrojf, the best keeper in the tournament, and
they actually took the lead after fourteen minutes through Josef
Masopust. Having held the South Americans to a 0–0 draw in
the group stages, there was hope Czechoslovakia could hold out
again, but there was too much talent in the Brazil side to be held
down for long. Amarildo — still white and Pelé-like — scored one
and set up another for Zito, and Schrojf made an uncharacteristic
error to allow Vavá to seal the deal at 3–1.

England 1966

In 1966, football came home. The founding fathers of the game,
England, triumphed on home soil in a tournament where no-
nonsense, practical European football triumphed over the skill and
flair of the South Americans. After winning two consecutive World
Cups, Brazil were quite literally kicked out of the tournament,
leaving hard-nosed England and West Germany to fight it out in
one of the most iconic — and controversial — finals ever played.

Coached by Alf Ramsey and playing a 4–4–2 formation that
earned them the nickname 'The Wingless Wonders', England's
style incorporated the tough tackling of Nobby Stiles with the grace
of defender Bobby Moore and the driving force that was Bobby
Charlton. An eight-month unbeaten run before the tournament
placed them as favourites, although Brazil, West Germany and
Portugal were all tipped to push them close.

Despite the top guns being on form, the biggest story from the early games was to come from the most unlikely of footballing nations: North Korea. Based in Middlesbrough and immediately taken to heart by the locals, North Korea shocked the world by beating mighty Italy 1–0, thanks to a goal from Pak Doo-Ik, sending the double world champions home in disgrace. Their stunning victory set up a quarterfinal clash against Portugal at Goodison Park, and North Korea did the unthinkable by going 3–0 up inside twenty-five minutes. However, the fairytale was soon over as Portugal stormed back to win 5–3, thanks to four goals from the irrepressible Eusébio (all scored before the hour mark, thank you very much).

Elsewhere, West Germany were efficiently progressing through the tournament and Argentina, when not receiving FIFA warnings for overzealous tackling, were proving to be a force too. The big upset was holders Brazil failing to make it to the knockout stage. With Pelé being kicked all over the pitch by opponents, a loss to Hungary — their first in the finals since 1954 against the same opponents — in the final group game meant that a hat-trick of titles was not to be.

The route to the final was littered with errant kicks, flailing elbows and sucker punches. West Germany played a quarterfinal against Uruguay and semifinal against the Soviet Union, and in both games their opponents ended the game with nine men. England and Argentina played out an equally unpleasant quarter, with Geoff Hurst's winner being overshadowed by the histrionics of Argentina captain Antonio Rattín (refusing to leave the pitch after being sent off) and Alf Ramsey branding his opponents 'animals'.

England's semifinal against Portugal was tame in comparison, with both sides deciding to play some football. Eusébio, who cemented his legend with a tournament-high nine goals and a string of dominating performances, couldn't breach the England defence, and in Bobby Charlton England had a match winner of their own. The comb-over superstar scored a goal in each half in a performance that confirmed him as the tournament's best player.

The final between England and West Germany was an entertaining affair, despite the two best players on the pitch — Bobby Charlton and Franz Beckenbauer — neutralising each other for much the contest. The game was in the balance until Martin Peters looked to have won it twelve minutes from time, but a free kick in the final minute saw Wolfgang Weber bundle the ball home and send the match to extra time.

And then it got interesting. Geoff Hurst thundered a shot against the bar and the ball bounced down on (or near) the goal line. After consulting with his Russian linesman, the ref awarded the goal — still the most debated in the history of the World Cup — before Hurst made sure of the result by smacking his third in at the death, as fans streamed onto the pitch thinking it was all over. The hat-trick was the first and still the only one to be scored in a World Cup Final, with England's three-goal hero finally getting to keep the ball thirty years later, after it was returned to him in 1996 by Helmut Haller, who nabbed it at the final whistle.

Mexico 1970

Viewed by many as the greatest World Cup ever, Mexico hosted a feast of skilful, attacking football the likes of which were never to be seen again (sniff). It was a finals full of iconic moments: Bobby Moore and Pelé swapping shirts after their group game, Gordon Banks's save in the same match, Brazil's brilliant fourth goal in the final, Beckenbauer playing the semifinal in a sling, and the enduring image of Pelé celebrating his first goal in the final, one arm in the air, as he is held aloft in the arms of teammate Jairzinho.

A successful tournament was by no means guaranteed, especially with players having to deal with the high altitudes and scorching midday kick-offs put in place to suit European TV audiences. Armchair fans were beamed live images in colour for the first time and were also introduced to three new phenomena that would stay with the game to the present day: the yellow- and red-card system of discipline, the use of substitutes, and a dedicated World Cup football: the black-and-white hexagoned and pentagoned Telstar.

The opening round started with a bang, as England and Brazil faced off in a marquee match featuring the two previous winners. Although Brazil emerged victorious thanks to a Jairzinho goal (he would score a goal in every game of the tournament), the match is best remembered for the 'greatest save ever': a diving Gordon Banks pawing Pelé's downward header up and over the crossbar. West Germany's Gerd Müller staked a claim to the Golden Boot, scoring successive hat-tricks against Bulgaria and Peru, while Italy advanced despite scoring just once in three group games.

The knockout stages were where this finals came to life. England and West Germany faced off in a 1966 final rematch; leading 2–0 in the second half, Alf Ramsey made a couple of puzzling substitutions (Hunter and Bell on for Charlton and Peters) and Germany pounced. Beckenbauer and Seeler took the game to extra time, where master poacher Müller scored a close-range volley to win the game. In other games, Italy found their scoring boots, beating hosts Mexico 4–1, and Brazil and Uruguay advanced against Peru and the Soviet Union respectively.

The game of the tournament saw Italy and West Germany play out a ding-dong semifinal at the wonderful Azteca Stadium. Italy's tried-and-trusted tactic of scoring and then retreating to protect a lead worked until the third minute of added time, when Karl-Heinz Schnellinger pounced to take the game to extra time. There the teams scored five goals, with Italy's Gianni Rivera netting the winner in a 4–3 thriller that also saw Germany captain Beckenbauer play much of the extra period with his arm in a sling for his dislocated shoulder.

Brazil were imperious on their route to the final, seeing off Teófilo Cubillas's Peru 4–2 and then exorcising the ghosts of 1950 by beating Uruguay 3–1 in the semifinal. That game witnessed the best goal never scored, a brilliant dummy by Pelé from a Tostão through-ball that left the Uruguay keeper in no-man's-land; with an open goal at his mercy, Pelé's shot ran across the goal and just past the far post. He was rubbish, that Pelé …

The final between Brazil and Italy was to decide the home of the Jules Rimet Trophy, as FIFA rules stated the first team to win it three times would keep it permanently. On paper the teams looked evenly matched, but in reality there was only going to be one winner. With a third winners' medal in his sights, Pelé opened the scoring in the eighteenth minute, and although Italy pulled level through Boninsegna, the South Americans dominated possession. In the 66th minute the floodgates opened, with Gerson and Jairzinho finding the net before Carlos Alberto scored a brilliant fourth. After threatening to quit the game after the 1966 tournament, 1970 was a fitting end to Pelé's career — and, despite his looming retirement, you would've been laughed out of Mexico if you said it would be twenty-four years before Brazil won another World Cup.

West Germany 1974

As was the case twenty years before, a West Germany led by a legendary captain triumphed over a side that arguably played the better football. Just as Fritz Walter's team shocked the Magical Magyars in the 1954 final, a Franz Beckenbauer–inspired West Germany triumphed over the 'Brilliant *Oranje*' of the Netherlands. However, unlike their first victory, West Germany were favoured to win the tournament this time around, not least because they were the hosts. With world-class players throughout the team, and in Gerd Müller a striker who was still knocking in goals for fun, West Germany were worthy winners and helped re-establish Europe as a footballing powerhouse.

Already European champions, West Germany were respected, but it was the Netherlands who were loved. Coach

Rinus Michels' team set the tournament alight from the very start, playing a style of Total Football that allowed players to switch positions and roles as the game unfolded. Relying upon a core of players from the dominant Ajax teams that had won multiple European Cups, including Johan Cruyff, Johan Neeskens, Ruud Krol and Johnny Rep, the Netherlands cruised through their side of the draw, accounting for heavyweights Uruguay, Argentina and Brazil on their way to the final.

The group stages went with the formbook, with first-timers Zaire, Australia and Haiti struggling to mix it with the big boys. David did triumph over Goliath in one group game though, as East Germany shocked their western compatriots 1–0 (although the defeat proved to be a shrewd move on the part of West Germany, as by finishing second in their group they avoided a second group featuring Brazil, the Netherlands and Argentina).

West Germany's steady march to the final continued in the second group, with wins over Yugoslavia and Sweden setting up a 'winner takes all' game against surprise package Poland. A tight affair was highlighted by the play of both keepers, with Germany's Sepp Maier pulling off some great saves in the first half and Poland's Jan Tomaszewski saving a penalty from Uli Hoeness. The match was decided fifteen minutes from time by — who else? — Gerd Müller, who pounced on a deflected shot from Hoeness to bulge the old onion bag.

There was no love lost between the two finalists, with many Netherlands players still able to remember the effects of German occupation on their families during the war. However, it was all business when the whistle blew (a little late, as ref Jack Taylor noticed there were no corner flags) and before West Germany had touched the ball, the Netherlands had put together a thirteen-pass move that resulted in Cruyff being fouled in the penalty area; Johan Neeskens converted the spot-kick to give the Netherlands the lead after just eighty seconds. The Netherlands' domination continued in front of a stunned home crowd, but

West Germany slowly came back into the game and they gained parity after winning a soft penalty on twenty-five minutes, which was duly despatched by Paul Breitner. No surprises that Gerd Müller got himself on the scoresheet to put West Germany ahead just before half-time, but it did come as a shock that the Netherlands couldn't find another goal in the second half, despite their all-out assault on Maier's goal. On his third attempt, classy German captain Franz Beckenbauer was finally a world champion, taking the honour of being the first captain to hoist aloft the brand-new World Cup trophy in front of the adoring home crowd.

Argentina 1978

The World Cup finals in Argentina was the most controversial since Italy in 1934 for what took place both on and off the pitch. It was common knowledge that the country was controlled by General Videla's brutal military junta, with stories of human rights violations, imprisonment, torture, 'disappearances' and murder engulfing the country in negative publicity. Neither FIFA nor the players were that bothered though — only Germany's Paul Breitner followed up on talk of a boycott by refusing to play — and Videla kindly agreed to not harm anyone for the duration of the World Cup finals to avoid further controversy.

On-pitch events were equally contentious, including drug bans, early final whistles (Clive Thomas blowing for time just before Zico's 'game-winning' header hit the back of the net) and the dodgiest of all dodgy games: Argentina vs. Peru. In that crucial group match, Argentina needed to win by four goals against their South American rivals to make the final — and they won by six. Immediately, talk of a fix emerged, with later reports uncovering a delivery of grain and arms to Peru from their grateful neighbours. The Peru game was just the biggest example of a tournament played in a hugely nationalistic atmosphere whipped up by

Videla, as rumours of intimidation and referee-fixing followed the host nation throughout.

Without an inspirational player or team emerging, the 1978 tournament brought few surprises or enduring moments. Archie Gemmill's brilliant individual goal against the Netherlands and the first win by an African nation (Tunisia beating Mexico 3–1) might have been memorable to Archie Gemmill's mum and a few North Africans, but a vintage finals it was not.

All the favoured nations progressed to the second group stage — the biggest surprise being undefeated Austria topping a group containing Brazil, Spain and Sweden — and it was at this stage that the games ramped up. In a quirk of scheduling the final group games had staggered kick-off times, giving those playing the later games the distinct advantage of knowing the results they needed. In Group A, it proved academic, as the Netherlands cruised to the final thanks to wins over Austria and Italy and a draw against West Germany, but in Group B it played a highly significant part in proceedings. Both Brazil and Argentina were on equal points entering their final game, and a 3–1 win by Brazil over Poland gave them a three-goal advantage over the *albiceleste*. But armed with the knowledge they needed to beat Peru by at least four, Argentina won by six and made the final; the result remains one of the most contentious in the history of the game.

The Netherlands had decided to refuse the trophy from General Videla if they won, but they needn't have worried — Argentina's name seemed to be already written on it. In an atmosphere the Netherlands' Johnny Rep later described as 'boiling', the South Americans started with a bit of mind games by complaining about a bandage worn by René van der Kerkhof; when the game finally started, it became obvious Argentina were going to counter the Netherlands' skill by kicking lumps out of them. But they were more than just thugs. The sublime Osvaldo Ardiles and Golden Boot winner Mario Kempes were worthy of any World Cup–winning side, and it was the latter who put his side in the lead on thirty-seven minutes. The Netherlands battled on for an equaliser that finally came from sub Dick Nanninga nine minutes from time, before Rob Rensenbrink hit the post with just a minute to go. But it was the closest the *Oranje* came, with Kempes and Daniel Bertoni finding the net in extra time to make the final score 4–2 to the hosts.

The final was equal parts triumph and tragedy, with Argentina finally reaching the pinnacle of the game after losing the very first World Cup Final in 1930 and the Netherlands losing a second consecutive final, one of history's greatest teams ending up empty-handed on the biggest stage.

Spain 1982

If the build-up to the finals in Spain was anything to go by, España 82 looked like it could be the most disastrous World Cup of all time. The acrimony started with the fact that many of the potential participants plain hated each other. Several countries complained to FIFA that England was a seeded nation despite not having played in the finals since 1970, with French coach Michel Hidalgo saying it was 'farcical that a nation which hasn't played in the finals for twelve years should be granted this privilege'. South American rivals Brazil and Argentina also entered into a war of words, with Diego Maradona claiming the draw would be rigged to help everyone's 'sweethearts', while Brazil responded with a call to ban the *albiceleste* after 'the fix' against Peru four years previous. Cameroon threatened to withdraw if New Zealand didn't condemn apartheid (the Kiwis had recently played against South Africa), Poland warned of 'riots in the streets of Warsaw' if they were drawn against the Soviet Union, and then there was the small matter of the Falklands War between England and Argentina. Who says sport and politics don't mix?

The host nation, Spain, were having troubles of their own. Newspaper *El Pais* called the finals 'the great national disaster' due to the chaotic state of its infrastructure, and the usually stuffy official draw in Madrid took on a comedic air when the ball-drawing machine jammed, Scotland were placed in the wrong group and a FIFA official shouted at one of the young Spanish orphans helping with proceedings to 'get it sorted out, boy!' live on air. Furthermore, the expansion of the tournament to twenty-four teams led to genuine fears that the smaller nations taking part — New Zealand, Kuwait, El Salvador — would provide little more than shooting practice for the more powerful nations.

However, when the tournament kicked off on 13 June in the Camp Nou, all was forgotten (well, maybe not the Falklands conflict, as England fans were beaten by Spanish police sympathetic to their Argentinean brothers) and the fans were treated to one of the most exciting tournaments in recent memory. Legends such as Platini, Zico, Zoff, Socrates, Maradona and Rossi all played starring roles, and it also bore witness to two of the best-ever World Cup games — the second-round group game between Italy and Brazil, and the semifinal between West Germany and France.

Brazil were most pundits' pick for champions, and for good reason. Featuring Zico, Junior, Socrates and Falcão, their XI was brimming with talent, and they made short work of their group, smashing four past New Zealand and Scotland. Rivals Italy got off to their usual slow start, only scraping through on goal difference after three draws, while Germany progressed thanks in no small part to the 'Game of Shame' against Austria, where the two teams played a highly uncompetitive final group game to ensure they both qualified at the expense of Algeria.

In the second group stage, all eyes were on the 'Group of Death', featuring Argentina, Brazil and Italy. The defending champs lost both of their games — with Diego Maradona red carded against Brazil — so the 'winner takes all' game between Brazil and Italy was touted as the game of the tournament. It didn't disappoint. Momentum swung in more directions than a sprinting dog's undercarriage and the match was finally edged by Italy, thanks to the brilliance of hat-trick hero Paolo Rossi. Favourites Brazil were out, and being known as the greatest team never to win the World Cup gave them little solace.

The semifinals saw Poland lose out to two Rossi strikes either side of half-time, but that game was a mere prelude to the epic that West Germany and France served up on 8 July. Tied at 1–1 at full-time, goals from Giresse and Trésor gave the French one foot in the final, but West Germany, inspired by the introduction of barely fit captain Karl-Heinz Rummenigge, clawed their way back to 3–3 and won the resulting penalty shootout. That the hero of the piece, German goalkeeper Harald Schumacher, should not have been on the pitch after his physical assault on Patrick Battiston, breaking his vertebrae and knocking out two teeth, only served to rub (garlic) salt in the French wounds.

Italy were favourites for the finals, but injuries to key players Antognoni and Graziani looked to have levelled the playing field somewhat. This was reinforced when Antonio Cabrini missed a penalty in the first half, but the irrepressible Rossi couldn't be held in check for long, and it was his header in the 57th minute that opened the floodgates. Goals from Marco Tardelli and Alessandro Altobelli followed, and a late Paul Breitner strike proved nothing but a consolation as Italy romped to their third World Cup title.

Mexico 1986

No player before or since has had such a singular impact on a World Cup finals than Diego Maradona in 1986. The mercurial genius from Buenos Aires wowed the world with his contentious mix of outrageous skills and outrageous gamesmanship. French newspaper *L'Equipe* called him 'half angel, half devil', and both sides were on show in Mexico as he inspired his Argentina side to victory.

Mexico were awarded the finals after Colombia had to pull out due to financial problems, but they had money issues of their own and had suffered a devastating earthquake that killed 25,000 people a year previous. The tournament was being played in the Latin American nation for the second time, and the second round was a straight knockout for the first time since the finals in 1970.

Several teams flattered to deceive early on. Denmark won all three group games, including a 6–1 dismantling of Uruguay and a 2–0 win over West Germany, but the 'Danish Dynamite' blew up in their faces in the knockout stage when they were thrashed 6–1 by Spain. The USSR, too, started well by smashing Hungary 6–0, but went the way of the Danes by losing 4–3 to Belgium in the second round. Slow and steady was the order of the tournament, with Italy and Argentina progressing from their group and England and France barely squeezing through after poor early results.

Penalty shootouts decided three of the four quarterfinals (West Germany over Mexico, Belgium beating Spain and France seeing off Brazil, after a scorcher of a match), while the tie that was decided in normal time proved to be one of the most memorable of all time, thanks to the genius of a certain diminutive Argentinean. Maradona's two goals against England embodied the 'half angel, half devil' perfectly. His first 'Hand of God' goal against a flailing Peter Shilton highlighted El Diego's *pibe* side — the fabled South American street kid who succeeds on his smarts and guile — while his second was all natural talent, slaloming past five defenders and slotting the ball under Shilton in what is universally accepted as the greatest goal ever scored.

Maradona's one-man show continued in the semifinal. Two brilliant individual goals saw off surprise package Belgium, setting up a final match-up against West Germany, who had quietly picked their way through the tournament with typical proficiency.

West Germany were able to keep Argentina's star player quiet for much of the final, but the *albiceleste* proved they were more than just Maradona by jumping out to a 2–0 lead with goals from José Luis Brown and Jorge Valdano. But the 'never say die' West Germany would not be put to bed so easily, and two goals in a six-minute period from Rummenigge and Völler evened things up with ten to go. Maradona's influence on the final came late, but when it arrived, it was decisive. With seven minutes remaining, his slide-rule pass sprung Germany's offside trap to send Jorge Burruchaga free to score the winner. Although the victory in the final was a team effort, very few captains have been more deserving of the honour of lifting the World Cup than Maradona in 1986.

Italy 1990

The events at Italia 90 speak much to the mystique and aura of the World Cup. Although the tournament was dominated by dour, negative and foul-filled performances, it is still looked back on fondly by those who recall the goal-scoring exploits of 'Totò' Schillaci, the tears of Gazza, the plucky Indomitable Lions of Cameroon and the lyrics to the ubiquitous *Nessun Dorma*. Sub-par football could do little to dampen the public's thirst for the World Cup; a cumulative TV audience of 26 billion watched fifty-two matches — twice the figure of those who watched Mexico 86.

The finals proved a mixed bag for the big footballing powers. Brazil and European champions the Netherlands both went out in the second round, and Argentina suffered a shocking opening-game loss to Cameroon in a game that featured one of the greatest fouls ever seen (Benjamin Massing clattered Claudio Caniggia so hard his boot flew off as he spun through the air). Italy, favoured to win the tournament on home soil, started superbly only to lose out to Argentina in a penalty shootout in the semifinal; England suffered the same semifinal fate at the hands of West Germany, after barely beating Belgium and Cameroon in the knockout stage.

The thrills and spills were left to one team making their first finals appearance and a striker who hadn't scored for his country before the tournament. Cameroon followed up their earth-shattering win over Argentina by topping their group and beating Colombia in the second round. Thirty-eight-year-old Roger Milla was the hero, twice coming off the bench in games to score a brace and then celebrating with a hip-swivelling dance around the corner flag. The Indomitable Lions' mix of skill and brute force won them many admirers, and if not for two Gary Lineker penalties in the final ten minutes of their 3–2 quarterfinal defeat to England, who knows how far they could have gone.

Italian striker Salvatore 'Totò' Schillaci was the standout individual in the tournament, with a rags-to-riches story to match. The scorer of a grand total of zero goals before the finals, he started the first game on the bench but ended up the winner of the Golden Boot with six goals to his name. The Italian public instantly took to the man from Sicily, and he became a cult hero who is remembered fondly to this day for his goalscoring exploits.

The 1990 final was definitely not one to remember, with Argentina going into the game with a record of a foul every four minutes. Both teams had the means and talent to make the game a classic — Germany with Lothar Matthäus and Jürgen Klinsmann at the top of their game, Argentina with Maradona and … erm … — but they decided cynical, negative football was what would win them the World Cup. Argentina's Pedro Monzón became the first player to be sent off in a World Cup Final after a lunge on Klinsmann, and Gustavo Dezotti felt so sorry that his teammate was in the changing rooms all alone that he later joined him for an early shower.

Thankfully, the world was spared another thirty minutes of extra time when Roberto Sensini fouled Rudi Völler and Andreas Brehme converted the spot-kick with five minutes remaining. The victory gave Germany its third world title and saw Franz Beckenbauer join Mário Zagallo as the only men to win a World Cup as a player and coach.

USA 1994

Although the USA were seen as deserving hosts — they had the stadiums and a massive sports-mad population guaranteed to fill them — there were more than a few concerns about giving the tournament to a country that seemed ambivalent about the beautiful game. The old joke went that 'Americans play soccer so they don't have to watch it', and a columnist for the *New York Daily News* summed up how many of his compatriots felt about the game when he said football was for 'Commie pansies'. Hell, they didn't even have a fully professional football league by the time the tournament kicked off ...

But against the backdrop of having a barely competitive national team and a media resistant to the idea of the finals, USA 94 was a success. Not that it was in doubt; FIFA wanted to break into the American market, and what FIFA wants, FIFA gets.

Like a Hollywood movie, the finals had a bit of everything: drama, tragedy, violence, farce, redemption and a gathering of teams and players that would make any A-list after-party. For drama, there was none other than Diego Maradona, playing in his final tournament, only to be kicked out for failing a drug test; tragedy, as Colombian defender Andrés Escobar was murdered outside a club in Medellín, some say for his own goal against the USA; violence, perpetrated by a host of players, including flying elbows from Brazil's Leonardo and Italian Mauro Tassotti; farce, in the shape of Diana Ross's horrendous penalty miss during the opening ceremony; and redemption for Brazil, who reached the pinnacle of the game for the first time since 1970. There were surprise performances from countries with no World Cup pedigree (Bulgaria, Romania, the USA), others relived the glories of yesteryear (Sweden), while for the big guns (Brazil and Italy) it was business as usual.

As for the men who made their mark during the summer of '94, it reads like a who's who of the greatest players of the decade: Jürgen Klinsmann, Cafu, Michel Preud'homme, Paolo

Maldini, Dennis Bergkamp, Roberto Baggio, Gheorghe Hagi, Hristo Stoichkov, Romário.

The group stages were full of surprises. Ireland beat Italy 1–0, Saudi Arabia triumphed over Belgium, and a Russian striker no-one had heard of, Oleg Salenko, scored a record five goals in a game against Cameroon. One of the pre-tournament favourites, Colombia, failed to make it out of their group and Italy only progressed from theirs by virtue of goals scored over Norway.

Bulgaria and Romania caused the shocks of the second round, beating Mexico and Argentina respectively. The latter was arguably the best game of the tournament, the sublime Gheorghe Hagi — 'The Maradona of the Carpathians' — elegantly controlling the game in the centre of the park and striker Ilie Dumitrescu scoring a brace.

In the quarters Italy beat Spain, Brazil saw off the Netherlands and Sweden needed penalties to see off Romania. The game of the round saw surprise package Bulgaria see off Germany, thanks to goals from Hristo Stoichkov and 'The Bald Eagle' Yordan Letchkov. Germany were favoured to win, especially after reunification, but the hard-drinking, cigarette-smoking Lions had too much heart and desire.

Any thoughts of a fairytale final between Sweden and Bulgaria were short-lived as traditional powerhouses Brazil and Italy made quick work of the pretenders to set up a rematch of the famed 1970 final. However, comparisons to that great game end there; the 1994 final was a turgid, snooze-inducing affair. Both teams were playing not to lose, and while Italy are well known for their *catenaccio* style, the dour, pragmatic approach of Carlos Alberto Perreira's Brazil team won him few friends, especially in his home country. The game had few chances in regulation, and penalties looked more inevitable than a Miley Cyrus stint in rehab. The first final to be decided on a shootout encapsulated the cruelty of the spot-kick decider, as missed penalties from Italy's two best players in the finals, Franco Baresi and Roberto Baggio, proved to be their undoing.

Brazil may not have won many fans along the way — striker Romário said the win was 'not the way the fans or me liked' — but winning that golden trophy still had their countrymen dancing in the streets to celebrate their historic fourth World Cup win.

France 1998

If the previous finals ended on a sour footballing note, then France 98 arrived with the promise of bigger and better things. A record 168 nations competed to qualify, and the tournament featured thirty-two countries for the first time in its history, meaning more games and a chance for first-timers such as Japan, Croatia, Jamaica and South Africa to make a mark on the world stage.

As the finals drew near, France was enduring a turbulent time both on and off the park. The country was riven by racial tension, the flames being fanned by right-wing leader Jean-Marie Le Pen, who said he did not recognise the French team as there were too many black players in the squad. On the pitch, the team had little form and the players were full of doubt and insecurity ahead of a pressure-filled finals. But, game by game, coach Aimé Jacquet's belief that his team would win the tournament began to take hold within the playing group. Not even the loss of talismanic Zinedine Zidane for two games — he was sent off for stamping in a precursor to his shocking head-butt in the 2006 final — could stop the French from storming their way to the final.

Not that it was plain sailing for *Les Bleus*, as the tournament featured several teams with aspirations of their own. After missing out in 1994, England were back and brimming with confidence; when coach Glenn Hoddle finally realised the bench wasn't the best place for David Beckham and eighteen-year-old Michael Owen, the Three Lions began to look like contenders. The same went for the Netherlands, who finally looked to have thrown off their infamous internal divisions to unite around the striking talents of Dennis Bergkamp and Patrick Kluivert. Romania were looking to back up a great performance in the USA, Germany and Italy were typically strong (although not at the peak of their powers), and Brazil were bringing a bit of their samba swag back with the phenomenal Ronaldo up front.

The surprise of the first round was the exit of Spain, victims of a slow start that not even a 6–1 final-game victory over Bulgaria could rectify. Other notable matches included the politically charged clash between the USA and Iran, the latter winning it 2–1, and a win by Norway over Brazil that featured a late, controversial penalty decision (later proved to be correct) for Norway.

The knockout round provided the usual exciting clashes, as newcomers Croatia beat Romania 1–0 and France scored the finals' first 'golden goal' to beat Paraguay in extra time. But the real fireworks took place at the Stade Geoffroy-Guichard when England faced Argentina. A feisty fixture at the best of times, the action on the pitch didn't disappoint, as two goals apiece in the first half — including an all-time great from just-out-of-nappies Michael Owen — saw the match poised on a knife-edge going into the second half, before David Beckham petulantly kicked out at Diego Simeone and was sent off. England played valiantly with ten men, but then came penalties. And we all know what happens when England, penalties and the World Cup converge ...

The quarters were part predictable (France and Brazil progressing) and part fucking awesome (Croatia stunning Germany 3–0, and Dennis Bergkamp's breathtaking winner against Argentina that made grown men soil themselves ever-so-slightly) and, after Brazil beat the Netherlands on penalties to reach a second consecutive final, it was down to France to book their date with destiny by beating Croatia 2–1. The brilliant

Croatia took the lead thanks to Golden Boot winner Davor Suker's second-half strike, but defender Lilian Thuram — a man who had never scored (and would never score again) for France in a 142-game international career — smashed two past Drazen Ladic to send *Les Bleus* into dreamland.

The final was full of intrigue and controversy before a ball had even been kicked. Brazil did not come out for their traditional on-pitch warm-up, and a team sheet was distributed with star striker Ronaldo's name omitted. A buzz quickly filled the stadium as word filtered from the press box to the fans, but suddenly a FIFA official grabbed the team sheet and replaced it with a new one with the striker's name now included. The reason behind the Ronaldo controversy was never fully explained (see Chapter 9 for more details), but it was obvious he wasn't the same player who had dominated games earlier in the tournament. Not that he would've been able to do much about a supremely confident France, who took control thanks to two carbon-copy headers from Zinedine Zidane and then weathered the sending-off of Marcel Desailly to win 3–0. With two heartbreaking semifinal defeats to their name, France had finally reached the top of world football. A million people flooded the Champs-Elyseés in celebration. Somewhere, Jules Rimet was smiling.

Korea/Japan 2002

The 2002 finals in Korea and Japan, the first held in Asia, showed that, as much as things change in football, they always stay the same.

Reputations were shown scant respect as a new generation of footballing nations emerged to take centre stage: goodbye Spain, Argentina and France — hello Senegal, Turkey and South Korea. Move over Raúl, Gabriel Batistuta and Thierry Henry; Papa Bouba Diop, Hakan Sukur and Ahn Jung-Hwan were the new kings in town. But as much as these industrious (and highly talented) nations shook up the tournament, the final was contested by the two most successful World Cup nations in history, Brazil and Germany, underlining that, no matter how hard you shake things up, the cream always rises to the top.

The finals felt its first seismic shock in the opening game when upstarts Senegal beat holders France thanks to a scrambled goal from the brilliantly named Bouba Diop; it was a defeat the French weren't able to overcome, as they exited the tournament without scoring a goal. Argentina, too, crashed out in the group stages after a 1–0 loss to England and a disappointing draw to Sweden. Elsewhere, the USA stunned Portugal 3–2 and qualified at their expense, while both host nations — Japan and South Korea — also emerged from their groups.

The surprise results kept on coming in the knockout stages as the USA, Senegal and Turkey all made it to the quarters and were joined by hosts South Korea, who shocked the world by beating Italy 2–1 after extra time. Guus Hiddink's Korea were super fit and highly organised (helped by the fact that the South Korean national league competition was suspended so the team had five months to train together), although their victory wasn't without controversy — Italy had a perfectly good goal disallowed and their star player, Francesco Totti, sent off.

Conspiracy theorists had a field day when Korea then went on to beat Spain on penalties (especially as Spain had two goals disallowed), although all that nonsense was put to bed when Germany beat them 1–0 in the semifinal. On the other side of the draw, Brazil were doing a good job of putting the 1998 nightmare behind them, confidently progressing to the final thanks to victories over Belgium, England and Turkey.

Due to the previous World Cup success of the two nations, a Germany vs. Brazil final had a familiar feel to it, although it was the first time the two countries had met in the showcase game. Brazil were powered by a rejuvenated Ronaldo who, after his disappointing final in France, bounced back to win the Golden Boot with eight goals. Supported by the skills of Rivaldo, the industry of

Gilberto Silva and the goofy, Jheri-curled artistry of Ronaldinho, the *Seleçao* were getting back to some of their best football.

The same could not be said for Germany, who looked dodgy in qualifying and entered the final off the back of three consecutive 1–0 wins and some stellar goalkeeping from Oliver Kahn. Their last two match-winners were scored by midfielder Michael Ballack, whose booking in the semi meant a suspension for the final. It proved a big loss.

Ultimately the redemption of Ronaldo proved too powerful for the Germans to resist, as the ridiculously coiffured striker scored twice in the second half to help Brazil take home their fifth world title and restore normality to the football world order.

Germany 2006

As if echoing its host nation's love of order and efficiency, the 2006 World Cup restored the balance of power to the established footballing nations. Events in Germany saw the usual suspects return to the top of the footballing pyramid: Italy won a fourth World Cup, thanks to teamwork and brilliant defending; France, led by many of their ageing stars, proved you can go a long way on a good French vintage; and Germany enjoyed a rejuvenation thanks to a dynamic coaching staff led by Jürgen Klinsmann, and a reliance on youth. That the Netherlands and Spain under-performed and England went out on penalties only confirmed the notion that normal service had been resumed.

For several of the big nations, the group stages were nothing more than training exercises. Brazil, Germany, Portugal and Spain won all three of their matches with ease, while Argentina looked the form team after a 6–0 dismantling of Serbia and Montenegro that featured probably the best team goal ever scored in the World Cup. In fact, Argentina were so strong that stars Lionel Messi and Carlos Tévez struggled to get a game — but with stunning strikes coming from the likes of Maxi Rodríguez in the Round of

16 against Mexico, there was little need. The exceptions to the rule were France, who snuck in behind Switzerland as runners-up, amid calls for coach Raymond Domenech to give youth a chance and let mercurial midfielder Franck Ribéry play from the start.

The Round of 16 threw up few surprises as Brazil (behind Ronaldo's World Cup–record fifteenth goal), Germany, Argentina, England, Portugal and Italy all triumphed, although the latter's win was more hard fought than expected, as a solid Australian side pushed them to the brink of elimination. Switzerland would feel privately aggrieved (although officially neutral) after losing to the Ukraine on penalties, becoming the first team to exit the World Cup without conceding a goal.

In the quarters England's latest excuse for not winning the World Cup — Wayne Rooney's sending off for a foul on Ricardo Carvalho — was wholly predictable, as was Italy's 3–0 win over the Ukraine. More surprising was France's 1–0 win over Brazil; France were thought to be a fading power, while Brazil were cruising through the tournament. But a flawless performance from Zinedine Zidane — all little flicks and perfect control — saw the holders go out with hardly a whimper. In the other quarterfinal, Germany beat Argentina on penalties after Miroslav Klose levelled the match ten minutes from time, and there were typical scenes of good sportsmanship and grace in defeat from Argentina at the final whistle.

While Zidane continued to inspire France, his penalty against Portugal sending their World Cup–winning old boys through to the final for a swan song, the second semi threw up a surprise result when Italy saw off hosts Germany. At 0–0, the game looked poised for penalties before a stunning, curling strike from Fabio Grosso won it for the Italians with just a minute to go; in added time, Alessandro Del Piero made sure with the last kick of the game.

The final was to become one of the most memorable in history, and not just for the football on show. Since Zinedine

Zidane had written his name so large on the tournament to that point, it was inevitable that he would be at the centre of the action come its conclusion. His impudent chip-shot penalty went in via the underside of the bar to give France a seventh-minute lead, but Marco Materazzi, who earlier gave away the penalty, made amends with a header on nineteen minutes to level the score. Chances were few and far between after that, the most notable falling to Zidane in extra time — but his header was pushed over the bar by Buffon.

As the game moved inexorably towards a penalty shootout, the two goalscorers had one last part to play in proceedings. After a brief coming together, Zidane jogged away from Materazzi, only to react to something that was said by turning around and launching himself headfirst at the Italian's chest. A red card followed for the French captain and, while the numerical disadvantage didn't harm the French for the remainder of the contest, it was an ignominious end to Zidane's career, and clearly rattled his teammates. In the shootout, France's David Trezeguet missed his side's fifth penalty and Fabio Grosso calmly slotted home to win the World Cup for Italy. The Italians triumphed due in large part to a stingy defence (only an own goal and a penalty conceded) and a team-first mentality that saw twenty-one of the twenty-three-man squad play a part on the pitch.

South Africa 2010

The decision to hold the 2010 finals in South Africa was shrouded in controversy even before the choice had been made. The Africans were supremely shafted when voting for the host of the 2006 finals was held in 2000 (see Chapter 10 for the full story) so, in 2004, FIFA decided the bidding process for 2010 would only be open to African nations.

South Africa saw off bids from Egypt and Morocco to secure the nineteenth World Cup finals, but there were huge concerns about safety, infrastructure, ticketing and travel leading up to the tournament. While the 'rainbow nation' had hosted many high-profile sporting events in the past — cricket tests and the rugby World Cup — nothing compared to a FIFA World Cup. A year out from the tournament, at the dry-run Confederations Cup, there were horror stories of journalists being robbed and bus drivers getting lost on the way to the grounds, and several stadiums were still unfinished. But, as was the case with previous World Cups beset by problems, the FIFA family ensured South Africa was ready by hook or by crook and, on 11 June, South Africa kicked off the tournament against Mexico at the terracotta pot–like Soccer City in Johannesburg.

The 2010 finals was a triumph of teamwork over the individual. It meant that nations building their team around one mercurial talent came a cropper, most notably England with Wayne Rooney, Portugal with Cristiano Ronaldo, and Argentina with Lionel Messi. Form and fatigue would play their part too, but the oppressive tactics employed by many teams meant that moments for superstar players to shine were few and far between.

In contrast, teams that focused on the power of the collective reaped the benefits. Top of the pile were reigning European champions Spain, whose ball-possession 'tiki-taka' style installed them as tournament favourites, although Germany's youth movement, led by tight-shirted coach Joachim Löw, were turning heads with some solid pre-tournament results too. Even the World Cup minnows proved that a well-drilled team could be a force to be reckoned with: New Zealand exited the finals without losing a game, Slovakia beat Italy in the final group game to make it to the Round of 16, and Ghana flew the flag for Africa by reaching the quarterfinals. Even North Korea scored against Brazil — not that anyone there got to see it ...

Other than Italy's early exit and some typically insipid performances from England (striker Wayne Rooney was caught by TV cameras swearing at England fans for booing the team at the end of the game against Algeria), the group stages provided few early surprises, while the Round of 16 winners read like a World Cup Hall of Fame, with five previous finalists (Uruguay, the Netherlands, Brazil, Argentina and Germany) joined by Spain, Paraguay and Ghana.

Germany reached their zenith in the quarterfinal against Argentina, dismantling Diego Maradona's men 4–0 (after a 4–1 tonking of England in the previous round), and the Netherlands raised a few eyebrows with a come-from-behind win over Brazil, thanks to two goals from pocket dynamo Wesley Sneijder. Spain squeaked past Paraguay 1–0 with a David Villa strike seven minutes from time, but it was left to Ghana's clash with Uruguay to provide more drama than the previous fifty-seven games put together.

The match was headed to extra time when Ghana had one last attack on Uruguay's goal. John Mensah's header was goalbound until striker Luis Suárez, standing on the goal-line, stuck up a hand (instinctively? cynically?) and parried the ball away. Time had run out and, after Suarez was sent off, Asamoah Gyan stepped up to take the spot-kick that would send Ghana to the semifinal. He hit the crossbar. Uruguay won the penalty shootout, and images of Suárez celebrating after his blatant cheating was seemingly rewarded gave fans a new public enemy number one. Not that there was time to hate the buck-toothed, baby-scaring cheat for too long, as four days later the Netherlands beat Uruguay 3–2 to book their place in the final. They were joined by Spain, who beat Germany in their third consecutive 1–0 match in the knockout stages.

Spain entered the final as favourites, dominating time of possession and passing their way through, around and past everyone they played (they would finish the tournament with 3500 passes completed). Xavi and Andrés Iniesta were masters of their craft in midfield, and in Carles Puyol and Gerard Piqué they had defenders at the top of their game. However, Spain often struggled to find the finishing touch to all their possession and, after David Villa's five goals, no other Spanish player scored more than one. This gave a sliver of hope to the Netherlands, who in Arjen Robben and Wesley Sneijder had match winners of their own.

Unfortunately, the Netherlands decided to adopt a game plan that led to the most negative, cynical and ill-tempered finals since the 1990 farce between Argentina and Germany. Firstly, the Netherlands' tactics seemed to centre around kicking seven shades of shite out of anything in a blue shirt, denying Spain their legs as well as any space to play. The Netherlands picked up nine yellow cards, including two for John Heitinga who was sent off in extra time, with the best/worst foul of the game coming in the shape of a studs-up kick in the chest from Nigel de Jong on Xabi Alonso. The *Oranje* also failed to take their one gilt-edged chance when it came, as at 0–0 midway through the second half Arjen Robben ran through on goal only to have his shot saved by the feet of Iker Casillas.

Spain were not without sin either, though, as they dished out some meaty challenges in retribution, but their talent shone through in the end — or, rather, *the very end*. As both sides tired with penalties looming, substitute Cesc Fàbregas latched onto a poor Netherlands clearance to put Andrés Iniesta through on goal, and the midfielder lashed his shot into the opposite corner past a helpless Maarten Stekelenburg.

There was no time for the Netherlands to respond and *La Roja* added the World Cup to the European Championship they had won in 2008. After adding a second European title in 2012, debate raged about Spain's place in the greatest national team of all time list; if they win again in Brazil 2014, it will be case closed.

2

THE EVOLUTION OF THE WORLD CUP

If you stood a fully kitted footballer from the 1930s and another from the 2010 World Cup finals next to each other, you would be hard pressed to guess who would fall on the floor first, doubled over in fits of laughter.

To the 2010 player, the 1930s version would look like a coal-worker going to participate in a sporting event at the bottom of a mine. With hobnail boots, oversized cotton shirts and shorts so baggy that you could fit Diego Maradona in each leg, it's a wonder the old guys could put one foot in front of the other, let alone coordinate complex footballing moves.

To the '30s player, the contemporary professional must look like some futuristic Flash Gordon uber-male, with pecs and six-pack bursting through a skin-tight shirt and sporting the kind of stupid Mohawk/hairband/ponytail (circle where appropriate) that would get you beaten up in a coalminer's bar.

Although it's easy to disregard the ability and achievements of the early footballer, every aspect of the game in the first World Cup — from what players were wearing and kicking to how they were punished for transgressions — made it infinitely more difficult to master. At the very least, having the nails holding the studs in your boots regularly pierce your feet would be a minor distraction to completing ninety minutes of football ...

As this chapter explains, modern footballers don't know how easy they have it; the World Cup has evolved a lot over eighty-four years.

Kits

Early football kits were made from cotton to withstand the physical rigours of the game, but this meant that in hot conditions they would become warm and heavy with sweat. Some teams experimented with shirts sporting latticed laces, or baggier shorts, but the evolution of the football kit was a slow process. It wasn't until the 1970s that kit manufacturers began to make shirts from synthetic materials that made them more comfortable to wear in the summer heat. (They helpfully saved on material by making budgie smuggler–sized shorts, too.) Some countries, most notably Brazil, kept their cotton shirts well into the 1980s, adding to their cool factor.

Modern-day World Cup kits are a licence to print money for global sporting manufacturers, who traditionally bring out new gear just before the tournament. Made from high-tech, sweat-wicking, lightweight materials — some of Nike's kits in 2010 were made from recycled bottles — modern shirts are typically tight-fitting (to show off the players' curves as well as making them harder to grab), much to the chagrin of the average pot-bellied football fan. Retro shirts are also popular, appealing to the fans' sense of nostalgia as well as patriotism; the 1966 red England, 1970 Brazil, 1978 Peru and 1986 Argentina are particularly iconic.

By the first World Cup in 1930, the majority of footballing nations had developed an identity through their kit colours — although some countries were willing to tweak things a little. Bolivian players emerged for their first World Cup game with Yugoslavia with a letter on the front of each of their kits that together spelt out 'VIVA URUGUAY' (although for their 4–0 loss to Brazil they would have been better off wearing 'NO MAS BRAZIL').

Brazil's own 'wardrobe malfunction' came after the 1950 final, when the pain of their shocking defeat to Uruguay led to them dumping their tainted white kit permanently. Brazilian newspaper *Correio da Manhã* ran a competition to design a new strip incorporating the colours of their flag (blue, green, yellow and white) and a nineteen-year-old named Aldyr Schlee emerged triumphant after entering as a joke.

Despite the colour of your opposition's shirts being common knowledge, there have still been a couple of high-profile kit clashes in the tournament. Brazil almost never made it onto the pitch for the 1958 final against Sweden after Sweden won the coin toss and elected to play in their home kit; *Seleçao* officials had forgotten to pack an alternative kit, and there was some hasty needlework needed to get the badges sewn onto some blue shirts.

'Someone was sent to get new shirts and then stuck the Brazil crest on them,' said defender Nilton Santos. 'We were already used to playing in the yellow shirts, but whether we win or we lose it's not because of the colour of the shirt.'

In 1978, both France and Hungary walked out onto the Estadio Mar del Plata pitch in white shirts; one of the teams should have been told to play in white, due to the TV broadcast being in black and white, but it seemed both teams were sent the same memo. The kick-off was delayed until local team Club Atlético Kimberley loaned the French their kit, although the less said about the green-and-white striped shirt, blue short combo the better …

And it would be remiss to not include some of the shocking kits to have graced football's showcase tournament too. Crimes to fashion included Cameroon's sleeveless numbers in 2002, the 1994 US kit with a terrible stars and stripes-over-denim motif, and anything worn by Mexican keeper Jorge Campos, who was given free rein by Umbro to design his own shirts, which looked like he swallowed a handful of glo-sticks and then puked them up onto some material.

Boots

It could be argued that the football boot has undergone a more radical evolution that any other tool of the trade. While the ball is still round, and the kit has maintained its shirt-and-short uniform, the boot has changed beyond recognition in the World Cup's eighty-four-year history.

Early boots were built more to protect the wearer than to enhance their ball control. Made from leather, and sporting steel toe-caps and high ankle protection, they were heavy to begin with, but doubled in weight when wet. There were small studs, or sometimes bars, that protruded from the sole in order to give traction in muddy conditions.

Boots became lighter and more flexible post-war, with the more familiar low-top look becoming more prevalent. Comfort was improved too, although clearly not enough for India, who pulled out of the 1950 finals when told by FIFA they were not allowed to play in bare feet. Technology advanced at a fast rate in the '50s, especially as the warring Dassler brothers — Adi at adidas, Rudolf at Puma — were trying to outdo each other at every turn. Adi gained the upper hand in 1954 when his revolutionary screw-in studs were said to have helped West Germany beat Hungary on a muddy Swiss pitch, although Rudolf would get his revenge when Puma-sponsored Johan Cruyff made the Netherlands produce a two-striped kit in 1974 so he didn't have to wear the rival three-striped brand.

Adidas Copa Mundials and Puma Kings were the standard-bearer shoes for nearly three decades (and are still the boot of choice for some old-school players) but the '90s saw two events that changed football boots forever. Firstly, US sportswear giant Nike came on the scene, producing the Tiempo range for the 1994 finals. Without the pedigree of the more established European brands, Nike relied on innovative design, fancy colours and aggressive marketing to grab a foothold, and is now the number-one retailer of football boots in the world. Secondly, the revolutionary adidas Predator was launched, a boot developed by former Aussie pro Craig Johnston that had rubber patches on the upper to improve power and control. Radical in itself, the shoe also changed the way footballers and consumers thought about boots and paved the way for all sorts of innovations in the decades that followed.

Nowadays boots are usually garishly coloured and customised for the feet of the top players (something that was once advertised but is now kept quiet from fans who are being sold on the comfort of boots straight out the box). The lightweight materials used have allowed boots to check in at under 200 grams a shoe, although there has been criticism that the lighter material has led to more foot injuries due to less protection. Make them all wear hobnail boots, I say ...

The World Cup football

While the outline of the World Cup football has remained the same — it's round, duh! — the design, materials and technology have undergone extensive overhauls over the years.

In the early tournaments, the ball was made of leather and constructed out of twelve panels, moving to an eighteen-panel design between 1954 and 1966. Each tournament's ball was produced by a supplier from the host country, leading to differences in performance, colour and shape from finals to finals. For example, in 1962 the Chilean ball did not meet European standards and, upon inspection ahead of the first match between the hosts and Switzerland, referee Ken Aston demanded a replacement ball after deeming all five match balls unplayable (the replacement finally arrived ten minutes into the second half). Balls from Europe were imported for the rest of the finals, but it didn't stop Brazil from winning the tournament.

From 1970 sportswear giant adidas secured the contract to produce World Cup footballs, and it was then that a series of iconic designs entered the footballing consciousness: the Telstar, with its mixture of pentagonal and hexagonal black and white panels, the Tango with its triangular 'triads', and the +Teamgeist, a slow-burning classic from the 2006 tournament. The materials developed along with the designs, moving from leather to a leather/synthetic mix to fully synthetic in 1986; things started getting stupid in the late '90s when phrases such as 'syntactic foam' emerged, and facts and figures about rigorous testing were thrown at fans who really didn't give a shit how many times the ball had been bounced to see if it retained its shape.

The World Cup ball reached its 'jumping the shark' moment in 2010 with the release of the Jabulani. Marketing babble droned on about the thermally bonded polyurethane-panelled balls being 'the most accurate and roundest' in history, but in reality it was pants. (Actually, a pair of pants would've flown straighter and truer than the Jabulani ball.) Both strikers and keepers united in their hatred of a supermarket ball that didn't fly right, Brazil keeper Júlio César calling it 'dreadful' and Italian striker Giampaolo Pazzini saying it was 'a disaster'. Even FIFA acknowledged there might have been a problem with the ball — scoring was down sixteen goals in the first round in 2010 compared to 2006 — but had more sense than to piss off adidas, one of their major sponsors, by pulling their flagship product mid-tournament. Because, of course, happy sponsors are more important than having a ball that works properly, eh?

December 2013 saw the release of the official World Cup ball for the 2014 finals in Brazil; the colourful Brazuca is named after the Brazilian word of approval for a skilful move and has already earned the seal of approval from the world's greatest player, Lionel Messi: 'I've had the opportunity to test Brazuca and it's great.' Surely it's just a coincidence that Messi is adidas's highest-paid sponsored player … ?

Yellow and red cards

Players being sent from the field of play for transgressing the rules have always been part of football. (The record books show that the first expulsion of the World Cup took place on the second day of the first tournament, when Peru midfielder Plácido Galindo was given his marching orders in the game against Romania in 1930.) But, due to the inherent issues with the language barrier between officials and players at an international tournament, many people either didn't know (Bobby and Jack Charlton only realised they had been cautioned in the 1966 quarterfinal when they were informed by officials the next day) or didn't care that they had been cautioned. (There are countless examples of players refusing to get off the field after being told to leave.)

It was the head of FIFA's Referees' Committee, Ken Aston — the man in the middle during the infamous 'Battle of Santiago' in 1962 — whose moment of inspiration at a set of traffic lights changed the world game forever. Already scarred by events in Chile — he never refereed another game — his frustration at player indiscipline reached boiling point during the 1966 quarterfinal between England and Argentina, when Antonio Rattín would not respond to the German ref who was sending him from the field. As Aston saw it, players were still not respecting the authority of the referees (which on some level is easy to understand, seeing as they're all complete wankers).

'I was driving home in my MG [*An unnecessary embellishment — PH.*] when the lights changed, so I slowed down and stopped,' recalled Aston. 'I didn't question the decision. So I thought that's it. Yellow for "take it easy", red for "stop". That's what football needs.'

His system of yellow and red cards was introduced in Mexico 70, and the first person to be shown a card (yellow) was Russian Evgeny Lovchev in the opening game against the hosts. The first red card was not shown until the following tournament, when Chilean Carlos Caszely kicked out at German Berti Vogts in 1974 and was expelled for his efforts.

Red cards have been handed out for a variety of reasons over the years, including 'violence of the tongue' (German ref Rudolf

Kreitlein's excuse for sending off Argentina's Antonio Rattín in 1966), laughing at a referee (the Netherlands' Dick Nanninga in 1978), using a WWE takedown move (Benjamin Massing on Claudio Caniggia in 1990), spitting into a mullet (Frank Rijkaard in 1990) and head-butting an Italian in the chest for saying bad things about someone's sister (Zidane on Materazzi in 2006).

Penalties

With the referee not on the pitch and the penalty kick yet to be invented, to the untrained eye football in the 1880s had the feel of a free-for-all bar brawl with a ball thrown in. But appearances can be deceiving; back in those turn-of-the-century days, the Corinthian ideal ruled: gentlemen would never lower themselves to commit a foul on an opponent, and the two captains would work out any on-field disputes amicably. (Captain one: 'Excuse me, but your defender just broke our striker's leg.' Captain two: 'Sorry about that, old chap. [*crack*] There you go — I've just broken mine, so now we're even.')

As absurd as it sounds in the 21st century, football players were pretty good at policing themselves in the early years of the game. However, as the stakes and the competitive nature of football rose, foul play began to creep in until the penalty kick — or 'the kick of death', as it was then known — was added to the Laws of the Game in 1891.

The first penalty scored in World Cup history was by Mexico's Manuel Rosas, who slotted home past Argentina's Angel Bossio on 19 July 1930; that it was the only penalty awarded in the finals is a little surprising, especially when you consider Uruguay and Argentina played in every game of the tournament. (Yeah, I said it.) The first penalty miss took place in the following tournament, when Brazil's Waldemar de Brito missed in Brazil's 3–1 loss to Spain on 27 May 1934. It proved to be a costly failure, as the *Seleçao* were knocked out of the tournament (1934 remains the only World Cup finals where Brazil failed to win a game), but de Brito made amends when he was a scout; he spotted a talented kid called Edson Arantes do Nascimento and took him to Santos to kickstart the greatest football career of all time.

The penalty shootout evolved in the 1970s as a means to decide tied games after extra time; replays were proving too difficult to arrange, and no-one was happy with the drawing of lots or tossing a coin to find a winner. The first major tournament to be decided on penalties was the 1976 European Championships final between Czechoslovakia and West Germany (look up 'Panenka' on YouTube for the coolest winning penalty ever scored), but the World Cup had to wait until the semifinal between France and West Germany in 1982 before it got to see its first shootout. (No game needed penalties in 1978, the first year the shootout was introduced to the tournament.)

Some teams have better luck with penalty shootouts than others. Top of the pile, unsurprisingly, are Germany, who have won all four of the shootouts they have been part of, while Argentina have a 75 per cent win rate (three wins, one loss). England has the worst record, losing all three of the shootouts they have been part of (1990, 1998, 2006) and scoring only 50 per cent of their spot-kicks. Italy were pretty poor too, going out of three consecutive World Cups on penalties (1990–1998) before finally winning one in the biggest game of all, the final against France in 2006. And spare a thought for the Swiss, the only team to take part in a World Cup penalty shootout and not score (0 for 3).

3

HOW TO WIN THE WORLD CUP

Okay, let's get the smart-arse answer out of the way first: the best way to win the World Cup is to win all your games by scoring more goals than your opposition. Yep, thanks for that. But, as anyone who has experienced the joy (and pain) of winning the World Cup can tell you, there's a little more to it than that. (Although former England striker Gary Lineker did have a point when he said, 'Football is a simple game: twenty-two men chase a ball for ninety minutes and at the end, the Germans win.')

The reality is that there is no master plan to winning the World Cup, no blueprint concocted by a football-coaching brain in a jar that will guarantee success. Why else would France get knocked out in the first round of the 2002 finals after winning the previous World Cup and European championships with virtually the same team? No two tournaments are the same, and a plan used by one coach to win the World Cup can lead to a first-round exit for another. Climate, injuries, team harmony, tactics, squad selection and media criticism are all variables that are completely out of the control of a team taking part, but how they deal with each one goes a long way to dictating whether their captain is standing with a giant gold trophy on the final Sunday or being bombarded by a silver-haired TV pundit demanding answers for another failed finals campaign.

Although I've never actually won the World Cup (and no-one has ever asked me how to either), this handy guide on how to win it is a great place to start for any national coach with aspirations to glory. Just remember to mention me in the post-match press conference if you manage to pull it off.

Don't lose your first group game

Without going all *Moneyball* on you, statistics show that if you lose your first group game, you might as well pack your bags and head home. Since the current group format came into effect in 1998, only 8.3 per cent of teams that lost their first game managed to claw their way into the knockout stage. The odds significantly increase if you draw your opener (58 per cent of teams progressed), while a win almost guarantees you a place in the knockout round (85 per cent). You definitely don't want to lose your first game if you're a seeded team; it's only happened twice, and neither country made it out of their group (Spain 1998, France 2002). Okay, you in the back — wake up, the maths lesson's over.

Get yourself a dictator

If American writer Henry D Fetter is to be believed, being governed by a dictator is virtually a prerequisite for World Cup success. Every winner of the World Cup in the last eighty years has been ruled by a dictator or authoritarian government at some point, with the exception of England in 1966. (Although Maggie Thatcher should count, shouldn't she?) Fetter noted that 'soccer prowess proved a national morale builder for the dictatorships of the last century', especially in the case of Mussolini's Italy (winners in 1934 and 1938) and for General Videla's military junta in Argentina in 1978.

The argument might be tenuous (I don't recall Xavi or Iniesta citing Franco as a factor in their 2010 victory) but don't bet against a desperate England allowing a totalitarian regime to come to power on the off chance it might finally bring another World Cup success.

Deal with missing players

During an arduous tournament where games against quality opposition come thick and fast, every team inevitably faces an injury or suspension crisis at some point. And it's how a team deals with their missing players that defines their tournament: Brazil lost their talismanic frontman Pelé to injury in 1962, but had the brilliant Garrincha to step into the breach and lead them to victory; in 1982 hugely influential Italian playmaker Giancarlo Antognoni missed the final, but coach Enzo Bearzot adjusted his line-up to include defender Claudio Gentile and the *Azzurri* hardly missed a beat.

But in the 1990 final, Argentina had to play without four key players, including top goalscorer Claudio Caniggia, due to suspension — and they were left severely lacking in an angry kickfest of a game. Armed with this knowledge, coaches have to make the all-important decision: replace missing players like-for-like, or adjust tactics and formation to accommodate their replacement? There's no right or wrong answer to this, but the coach who doesn't evaluate the men he has at his disposal accurately will find himself making an early trip home.

Pick the right food

It's common knowledge that nutrition is key to an athlete's performance, but during a World Cup it's not all about electrolyte drinks and energy gels. Three square meals a day are also needed to keep the players nourished and, if you get it wrong, then it's not just stomachs that will be upset.

Let's take a look at two teams' chow choices to see how things can go either way in the culinary stakes: in 2006, Italy ate their way to a world title with a staple of traditional dishes — 'I stuck to the classics: *risotto alla parmigiana, cosce di pollo arrosto e branzino al rosmarino al forno*, roast potatoes and *crostata*,' revealed Italy's official chef Claudio Silvestri to

FourFourTwo — while in 1970, England struck a deal with frozen food company Findus and lived on a diet of fish fingers after Mexican customs seized the majority of their food consignment from the cargo boat. They didn't make it past the quarters. And so the famous phrase * was spawned: 'You don't win the World Cup on fish fingers alone …'

Put the emphasis on 'team'

The pressures and strains of the World Cup are not just confined to matters on the pitch. Players and coaches have to live with each other in close quarters for around two months (if you count pre-tournament training camps) and, if the group dynamic isn't just right, then a tournament can be over before it begins. Eradicating jealousy, egos and club rivalries might be easier said than done, but if you can get your squad to forget their differences for the greater good, then harmony on the pitch is achieved more easily.

Italy's World Cup–winning coach Marcelo Lippi put it this way:

> **I'm not convinced I brought together the technically best players I could have. But I was convinced I called the ones that could create a team and play for one another.**

Avoid Germany

Whether it's in the group stages or knockout rounds, your best chance of hoisting the World Cup trophy aloft at the end of July is to avoid Germany. If your team is drawn in the same group as *die Mannschaft*, consider that they have made it out of every group stage since 1954, only failing to top the table in 1974, 1978 and 1986 (and in '74 they deliberately finished second to avoid the stronger group in the next round). With Germany almost

---

* This may or may not be a famous phrase where you come from.

inevitably winning the group, the best-case scenario is then a second-place finish and a Round of 16 match against another group's winner.

Facing them in the knockout stages is no easier, though; other than two quarterfinal exits in 1994 and 1998, Germany have made at least the semifinals in every World Cup since 1982. Finally, don't even bother taking part if it comes down to a penalty shootout. In four World Cup shootouts, they have taken nineteen penalties and only missed one (Uli Stielike in 1982 against France). *'Vorsprung durch Technik'* indeed.

Don't get involved in a classic

Although edge-of-the-seat comebacks or extra-time slugfests might keep the fans entertained, it is almost certainly a suicide mission for the victorious team. Throughout the tournament's history, teams that have triumphed in classic World Cup final matches have gone on to lose their following game: Hungary in 1954 (beat Uruguay in the semi, lost to Germany in the final), Portugal in 1966 (beat North Korea in the quarters, lost to England in the semi), Italy in 1970 (beat West Germany in the semi, lost to Brazil in the final), West Germany in 1982 (beat France in the semi, lost to Italy in the final) and Argentina in 1998 (beat England in the Round of 16, lost the quarterfinal against the Netherlands). The expenditure of energy in those classic matches usually means there's little left in the tank for the rest of the tournament. So if you're a couple of goals down or heading into extra time, you're better off not making the effort ...

Handle adversity

Adversity can come in many guises during a World Cup campaign: a shock result, poor performances, criticism from the media, divisions within the playing group and any number of scandals involving chemicals or errant genitalia. Some difficulties prove too hard to overcome, both on and off the pitch, but many of the most successful teams turn adversity to their advantage, creating a 'them against us' siege mentality that serves to galvanise the playing group.

Over the last two decades, several teams have used that technique to spur them on to victory: the 1982 Italy, 1986 Argentina and 1994 Brazil teams all triumphed despite heavy criticism from their home press for poor results and negative playing style. Aimé Jacquet united his France team against a media that was calling for his sacking before the 1998 tournament had even started and, in 2006, Italy became champions against the backdrop of a match-fixing scandal that directly affected several members of the squad.

Don't be picked by Pelé to win it all

Pelé: brilliant footballer, crap pundit. It's understandable that journalists would look for the opinion of the world's greatest player for all things World Cup, but getting Pelé's seal of approval is a sure-fire way to not win the tournament. Here are just a few of his off-target predictions: he said Colombia would make at least the semis in 1994 (they finished bottom of their group), Spain were his favourites in 1998 (they crashed out in the group stage), Argentina and France would contest the 2002 final (both went out in the first round) and an African nation would win the World Cup before the year 2000 (no African nation has made it past the quarters).

His eye for talent is not much better, picking Ghanaian Nii Lamptey (who?) as the 'new Pelé' after the 1997 U17 World Cup and declaring England's Nicky Butt as the best player in the 2002 World Cup. (WTF, as the kids like to say …) Summing up Pelé's punditry skills, Brazil legend Romário once said: 'When Pelé is quiet, he's a poet. But he just talks shit.'

Take England or the Netherlands to penalties

On paper, drawing England or the Netherlands in the knockout stages of the World Cup might present a few problems — but these two nations are actually the easiest touches in the history of tournament football ... if you can just take them to a penalty shootout. Of course, repelling wave after wave of *Oranje* attacks or staving off a rabid ten-man England (after the obligatory sending-off, which will later fuel their sense of injustice at being knocked out) for 120 minutes isn't easy, but if you can last out until spot-kicks then you're pretty much through. England have lost all three of their World Cup shootouts (and two of three in the Euros), while the Netherlands have lost one shootout in the World Cup (and three of four in the Euros). Even Pelé might be able to predict the winner with those kinds of odds ...

4

WORLD CUP LEGENDS

When you think about it, becoming a famous footballer isn't that hard. Play long enough in one place or score a goal of some significance (a 30-yard screamer against a cross-town rival, a toe-poke to win the cup, a last-minute strike to avoid relegation) and a savvy ex-pro is pretty much guaranteed to never have to buy a drink in town again. They'll be rolled out for speaking engagements at the end-of-year awards nights, have a charity golf tournament in their name and be called in to give their bland opinions on TV when their former club has a live game on TV. Life's good for a celebrated ex-footballer.

However, there is a select group of players who reach a level of fame and regard that few can envisage. In fact, it's possible even they could never have imagined that they would one day be regarded as the very best footballers the world has ever seen: World Cup legends.

Numerous men have played significant roles in the development of the World Cup as a sporting event, inspired their team to the pinnacle of the game, or seen the best four weeks of their footballing career coincide with the world's greatest football tournament. But a true World Cup legend has achieved all three, and then some …

Nailing down the definition of a World Cup legend is fraught with danger. Does a legend have to have won the World Cup? Do they at least have to have played in multiple tournaments? Is it just about what they achieved on the pitch? (The short answer to that is: no, no and no.) I decided that a legend of the World Cup is a player who cemented his legacy by his performances, influence and accomplishments in the World Cup; regardless of the rest of his career, his greatest footballing achievements took place in the World Cup finals.

Like all good teams, some players picked themselves (Pelé, Maradona), while others were more contentious selections (Just Fontaine and Johan Cruyff played only thirteen World Cup games between them), but, like any good coach, I stubbornly stick by my selections.

It's an eclectic bunch, from multiple tournament winners and World Cup record breakers to nationality-changing hard men and men with nicknames like 'The Rubber Man', 'The Black Panther', *'Der Kaiser'* and *'O Fenômeno'*. But first, the man who made it all possible …

Jules Rimet

When Frenchman Jules Rimet boarded a steamboat on its way to the first World Cup in Uruguay in 1930, he carried the World Cup trophy in his hand luggage. No security guards, no cotton gloves, no replicas to put thieves off the trail; just one man with a 30-centimetre golden statuette of Nike, the Greek goddess of victory, in his bag. In many ways, the trophy and its journey represented Rimet's fledgling tournament; although undeniably attractive, both were low-key and built on a small scale, giving no hint of the global icon they would soon become.

The son of an immigrant greengrocer, Rimet was a lawyer by trade — but he had football in his heart. He was instrumental in advancing the professional game in France, and was at the forefront of the creation of the first world governing body for football, the Fédération Internationale de Football Association (FIFA), in 1904. After fighting with distinction in WWI, Rimet became FIFA president in 1921 and, with the lines between amateurism and professionalism in the game becoming increasingly blurred, he pushed forward with the idea of a fully professional world football championship, the World Cup. His idea came to fruition in 1928 with the announcement that the first finals would be held in Uruguay, where the government happily offered to bankroll the entire event.

Although Rimet was an idealist who saw the World Cup as a means to promote hard work, integrity and fair play among its competitors, he was still canny enough to ensure FIFA would take 10 per cent of the profits from the tournament. (Can you hear that? That's the sound of current FIFA president Sepp Blatter's head exploding at the naivety of securing 'only' 10 per cent of the profits ...)

Under Rimet, the World Cup became the global sporting event he envisaged, especially when the petty in-fighting between European nations ended and the tournament was truly contested by the best footballing nations in the world — even England bit the bullet and participated for the first time in 1950. But his finals weren't without controversy, especially those marred by overt displays of National Socialism in the 1930s, as FIFA were viewed as complicit in proceedings. In fact, Rimet's turning a blind eye to the shameful antics of Mussolini during the 1934 finals was said to have cost him a chance of winning the Nobel Peace Prize; the jury rejected his nomination in 1956.

While the Frenchman would come to understand the impact of his creation by the time he stood down as FIFA president in 1954 — the trophy he had carried twenty-four years earlier by then bore his name — he would've been shocked by how the modern World Cup has evolved.

'[He] believed that sport could unite the world,' said Yves Rimet in an interview with *The Independent* in 2006, on the fiftieth anniversary of his grandfather's death.

Unlike many others in his time, he realised that, to be truly democratic, to truly engage the masses, international sport must be professional. All the same, my grandfather would have been disappointed with the money-dominated business that football has become. That was not his vision.

Luis Monti, Argentina 1930, Italy 1934

Argentinean defender Luis Monti was not going to let anything get in the way of him becoming a World Cup winner — not even his own nationality. After playing in the loss to Uruguay in the first final for Argentina, he switched allegiances to Italy and was an integral part of the triumphant 1934 team, becoming the first and only man to play in consecutive finals for different countries.

Monti was a tough, uncompromising and oftentimes violent footballer who would stop at very little to achieve his ultimate aim: winning football games. A much-told story about the Argentinean had him holding out his hand to shake with a Chelsea player during a friendly, only for him to pull it away and kick his opponent instead. However, the original 'midfield hardman' was more than just a hatchet man; he was also technically gifted, a great passer, and earned the nickname *doble ancho* (double wide) for ~~his big arse~~ the prodigious amount of turf he covered during games.

Monti's journey from Argentina to Italy began in Uruguay at the first World Cup Final. As the most prominent member of the Argentina team — both for his skill with the ball and his prowess at injuring opponents — he became a hated figure to rival fans and, ahead of the final in Montevideo, he was the victim of death threats from both sets of fans: the Uruguayans told him he'd be killed if he won the game, and the Argentineans said he'd be killed if he didn't. Only comforting words from team officials stopped Monti from pulling out of the game entirely, but the threats clearly shook him. He had his worst game of the tournament and was said to have told his teammates at half-time that he didn't want to become a martyr over a football game. His abject performance was roundly criticised in the Argentinean press — they dubbed him a 'coward' — and the blame for the defeat was laid firmly at his doorstep.

An outcast in his own country, Monti opted to move to Italy, where Juventus were more than happy to use a man of his talents. He helped 'The Old Lady' win four Scudetti in five years, and when Italian coach Vittorio Pozzo announced his intention to select *oriundi* — foreign players of Italian descent — for his World Cup team, the thirty-three-year-old jumped at another chance of winning the World Cup. And he did just that, bossing the *Azzurri* midfield with his blend of skill and subterfuge as the Italians romped to a 2–1 victory over Czechoslovakia in the final.

The death threats from the first World Cup Final still played on Monti's mind many years later, as he said in an interview with a certain amount of gallows humour:

> **I had to win that game. If I had won in the 1930 final the Uruguayans would have killed me. And if I had not won in the 1934 final the Italians would have killed me!**

Giuseppe Meazza, Italy 1934, 1938

Giuseppe Meazza was the first phenom of world football. Regarded as Italy's greatest-ever footballer, the Inter Milan attacker was blessed with the holy trinity of pace, vision and technique — and was a lethal goalscorer to boot. But, unlike many stars whose personal ambition leads to an egotistical streak, Meazza was also a selfless creator, helping fellow Italy forwards Angelo Schiavo, Giovanni Ferrari and Silvio Piola to a glut of goals during their careers.

Meazza had no equal in the 1930s, a decade that saw him win three Scudetti, top the Serie A goalscoring table four times, and win the World Cup in 1934 and 1938.

Born in Milan in 1910, Meazza had a tough childhood — his father died in WWI and his mother opposed his footballing ambitions — but there was no stopping 'Peppino' from fulfilling his destiny, and he signed with Inter Milan as a skinny fourteen-year-old. He played his first game for the *Nerazzurri* as a seventeen-year-old in a pre-season tournament and promptly scored two in a 6–2 win, going on to score twelve goals in thirty-three games in the 1927–28 season. In his second campaign, he hit thirty-one goals in thirty-three games — including a hat-trick in the opening four minutes against Roma — and a star was born. International recognition came soon after and the goals kept flowing: two on his debut versus Switzerland, and a hat-trick against Hungary. Before his twentieth birthday, Meazza had scored ten international goals in just seven games.

Considering the Inter man was clearly a goalscoring prodigy, Italian coach Vittorio Pozzo's decision to move Meazza to inside-right to accommodate Angelo Schiavo ahead of the 1934 World Cup finals was a bit of a head scratcher. But, rather than gripe about being played out of position, the twenty-four-year-old transformed himself into the master creator. While his goal tally dwindled in the tournament, his contribution was still decisive; he scored the only goal against Spain in a quarterfinal replay but, more importantly, set up the winner in the semifinal against Austria and was instrumental in the lead-up to the winning goal in the final.

In 1938 Meazza was still a force to be reckoned with — he scored twenty-eight in thirty that season — and he was made captain of his country for their defence of the world title. Meazza linked up with a new strike partner, Silvio Piola, and the two combined to devastating effect. He may have scored only one goal — a penalty against Brazil in the semifinal — but he set up the majority of Piola's chances (who scored five times in the tournament) and played a hand in three of the four goals Italy scored in their 4–2 victory over Hungary in the final.

One downside to Meazza plying his trade in the 1930s is that there's little archival footage of him playing, which is a shame as the stories of his goals are the stuff of legend. Having previously scored an overhead kick against keeper Gianpiero Combi in national team training, the Juventus stopper bet Meazza he couldn't do it again in a game; despite the entire Juve team knowing what he was going to try, they couldn't stop him from finding the back of the net and winning the wager. Equally fabled is his goal in a friendly against Austria in Rome in 1936; advancing on goal with a defender running at him from either side, Meazza abruptly stopped with the ball and the two defenders ran into each other, Tom and Jerry–style. With his opponents flailing on the ground, he breezed past the keeper to score with ease.

Meazza likened his playing style to a lazy tiger who feigns disinterest before leaping upon his prey:

> **Opposing teams often assign two or three people to mark me. I never yearn for solitude more than in these matches, so I act like I'm not interested in the game. And then I pounce.**

Meazza pounced thirty-three times in fifty-three games for Italy before retiring from the game in 1947, going on to coach Atalanta, Inter and the national team between 1952 and 1953. An Inter Milan legend, who also played a couple of seasons for rivals AC Milan, Meazza was held in such high regard that, upon his death in 1979, both clubs agreed to officially rename their San Siro Stadium as the Giuseppe Meazza Stadium in honour of Italy's best ever.

Leônidas, Brazil 1934, 1938

> **He was as fast as a greyhound, as agile as a cat, and seemed not to be made of flesh and bones at all, but entirely of rubber. He was tireless in pursuit of the ball, fearless, and constantly on the move. He never conceded defeat. He shot from any angle and any position, and compensated for his small height with exceptionally supple, unbelievable contortions, and impossible acrobatics.**

Writer Jerry Weinstein's brilliant observation of Brazil's Leônidas da Silva failed to mention only one thing: the way his dazzling skills and childlike enthusiasm captured the imagination of fans in the 1938 finals to such an extent that he can rightly be called the World Cup's first superstar. Known both as 'The Rubber Man' and 'The Black Diamond', his outrageous skill and gravity-defying contortions made him an immediate fan favourite all over Brazil, and he increased his popularity tenfold when he took the 1938 tournament in France by storm, putting in Man of the Match performances on the pitch and Man of the People displays off it.

Emerging from the Rio streets where he learnt to play barefooted, Leônidas signed with local club Sirio Libanes at sixteen before playing for Bonsucesso, Penarol and Vasco da Gama — all before he was twenty-two. He may have bounced around from team to team in his club career, but Leônidas was firmly established as a member of the Brazil team in the early 1930s, his standout performance being two goals as a nineteen-year-old in a win over world champions Uruguay in 1932. He was selected for the 1934 World Cup finals, but a disjointed Brazil side struggled in their opening match against Spain and, due to the knockout nature of the tournament, the *Seleçao* were sent packing back to South America after just ninety minutes.

The 1938 Brazil team was altogether more coherent, and Leônidas lay down a marker in the very first game, scoring a hat-trick (and many argue a fourth too) in the legendary 6–5 extra-time win against Poland. 'The Rubber Man' was virtually unstoppable in that game, with two extra-time goals that some reports say were dispatched bootless, after the Brazilian threw his shoes away to gain better traction on the muddy pitch (although the more likely story is they fell off in the terrible conditions). With or without boots, Leônidas became an overnight sensation, adding to his goalscoring tally with a strike in both games against Czechoslovakia, a brutal 1–1 draw and a more easygoing 2–1 replay win.

Then came one of the most baffling decisions in World Cup history: Brazil coach Adhemar Pimenta's decision to rest Leônidas for the semifinal against Italy. Whether Pimenta was saving him for the final or allowing him to recover from an alleged thigh injury, leaving out his best player against the defending world champions proved disastrous, as the *Azzurri* triumphed 2–1. Leônidas did find the scoresheet twice in the third-place playoff match, meaning he at least returned to Brazil with the Golden Boot award for his seven goals.

Leônidas was the most famous man in Brazil upon his arrival home and he continued playing for another twelve years, winning several titles with Flamengo, despite an ongoing problem with his knee. In retirement, he worked as a coach, private detective and radio commentator (imagine his LinkedIn connections!) and, despite passing away in 2004 after a long battle with Alzheimer's disease, his name lives on in Brazil in the form of a famous chocolate bar, *Diamante Negro* (The Black Diamond), which is still sold today.

Just Fontaine, France 1958

French striker Just Fontaine's stunning thirteen goals in six games during the 1958 finals — a record that still stands today — would seem to be written in the stars if not for two tiny facts: as the tournament kicked off in Sweden, he was not France's first-choice striker — and he didn't have a pair of boots.

Moroccan-born Fontaine had a formidable reputation as goalscorer, his short, stocky frame, tree-trunk legs and low centre of gravity making him the perfect 18-yard box goal poacher. He scored more than 120 goals in six seasons for Reims, and between 1957 and 1960 did not finish outside the top two on the French league's goalscoring charts.

But despite scoring thirty-four goals en route to winning the Double with Reims in 1958, he wasn't guaranteed a starting spot in the France line-up, competing with René Bliard for a place up front with the brilliant Raymond Kopa. Fate stepped in when Bliard was injured in a warm-up match. For Fontaine, the only thing that stood between him and his date with destiny was a pair of boots, as his own had sheared away at the sole.

'We only had two pairs at the time, and no sponsors,' said Fontaine. 'I found myself with nothing. Luckily, Stéphane Bruey, one of the second-choice strikers, wore the same size as me and lent me his boots.' The rest, they say, is history.

Scoring in all six games he played, the twenty-four-year-old started things off with a hat-trick in a 7–3 win against Paraguay, two in a loss to Yugoslavia, and one in a 2–1 win against Scotland. Fontaine and Kopa combined amazingly well, enjoying the kind of telepathic understanding that comes once in a lifetime: 'Justo was the striker who best suited my style of play,' said Kopa. 'He knew exactly what I was doing and I could be sure of finding him at the end of one of my dribbles.'

Fontaine scored twice in the 4–0 quarterfinal win against Northern Ireland and another in the 5–2 semifinal loss to eventual champions Brazil, leaving him needing a hat-trick in the third-place playoff to beat Sándor Kocsis's record of eleven. In a game not traditionally known for its competitive nature, Fontaine scored four against West Germany, giving him outright ownership of the scoring record with thirteen goals. At the end of the tournament, Fontaine gave the record-breaking boots back to Bruey:

> **I gave them back. I like to think some of my goals were inspired by combining two spirits inside the same shoe … [but] they didn't make him score more goals.**

A disappointing footnote is that Fontaine didn't receive a Golden Boot Award for his achievement; all he got was a symbolic rifle from a local newspaper (although England striker Gary Lineker did present him with one later as part of a UK TV program).

Fontaine played his last game for France against Bulgaria in December 1960, struck down at just twenty-seven years old with a double fracture of his leg that proved too big an obstacle to come back from. Not just a goalscoring flash in the pan, the Frenchman's strike rate for club and country was as good as any in the game, but it's his haul in '58 that is most likely to stand the test of time. As the man himself said, with typical Gallic modesty: 'Thirteen goals is an enormous total. Beating my record? I don't think it can ever be done.'

Pelé, Brazil 1958, 1962, 1966, 1970

Football video games have long given players the ability to create their own footballers, allowing light-sensitive geeks with questionable social skills the opportunity to make an all-conquering player with the highest possible attributes: 100/100 shooting, 99/100 pace, 99/100 passing, 98/100 dribbling, 100/100 scoring with hand while referee looks the other way … This feature always seemed against the spirit of the game, a bit like creating a Lance Armstrong of football, but more importantly it was also completely pointless as there was already a footballer who possessed those ridiculous numbers: Pelé.

Edson Arantes do Nascimento was the perfect footballer. If you listed the qualities a truly great footballer should be endowed with, Pelé had them all: pace, strength, tactical nous, trickery, skill, intelligence and the ability to score with any part of his body. Pelé ushered in a golden age of football for Brazil and helped establish them as the number-one footballing nation in the world, winning the World Cup in 1958, 1962 and 1970. No wonder he is known in his home country by the simplest of nicknames: 'O Reï', 'The King'.

Although the record books show he was a three-time World Cup winner, the reality is Pelé only played a significant part in winning the first and last tournaments he played in. In 1962 he was injured after the second group match and had to watch his country's victory from the sideline, while in 1966 he was literally kicked out of the tournament by his opponents. But even Pelé's World Cup lows play a significant part in his story and, similar to the careers of other sporting greats such as Muhammad Ali, Michael Jordan, Greg LeMond and Niki Lauda, his triumphant return to the peak of his profession only serves to strengthen his legend.

Pelé was a recordbreaker before he even took the field in the 1958 World Cup. In his debut against Argentina the previous year, at sixteen, he became the youngest player to score an international goal. The European football audience was eager to see what all the fuss was about, but they had to wait until the final group game to get a glimpse of the superstar-in-waiting. A knee injury kept the young phenom out of Brazil's first two games but, at the behest of senior players eager to light a fire under the team in a crucial win-or-go-home match, Pelé — and mercurial teammate Garrincha — started against Russia. It was worth the wait. Both players hit the post in the first two minutes and inspired their country to a 2–0 win.

The deadly duo weren't left on the bench again. Despite concerns he might not last the rigours of a long, tough tournament, Pelé not only proved durable, but quickly became the team's driving force. He scored the winner against Wales (becoming the World Cup's youngest scorer, at seventeen years and 239 days) and added a hat-trick in the semifinal against France. In the final against hosts Sweden, he scored two more: a volley after a cheeky flick over the last defender, and a beautiful looping header to seal the game. Even the Swedish players were impressed, one saying: 'After the fifth goal, I felt like applauding.' Brazil had finally won the World Cup, and an emotional Pelé had to be comforted by his teammates after breaking down in tears on the pitch.

Although Brazil defended their title in 1962, it was without much of a contribution from Pelé. Struggling with a thigh injury on the eve of the tournament, Pelé kept it quiet due to coach Vicente Feola's policy of picking only fully fit players, but the leg lasted only two games. Things didn't get much better for Brazil's No.10 in 1966, as he became a marked man in every game he played. Not given the necessary protection by the referees, he was kicked from pillar to post by the opposition — receiving particularly rough treatment from Portugal — and he left the tournament a broken man. Hacked off in both senses of the word, 'O Rei' vowed never to play in the World Cup again, not wanting to end his career 'as an invalid'.

Luckily, Pelé didn't follow up on his threat, and the 1970 finals in Mexico proved to be his crowning glory. Ably assisted by the talents of Jairzinho, Tostão, Gerson and Rivelino, Brazil put in a performance for the ages, beating England 1–0 in a group game that many saw as a dress rehearsal for the final, and exorcising the ghosts of 1950 by beating Uruguay 3–1 in the semifinal.

Pelé scored four goals in the tournament, but his influence was more than just on the scoresheet. It was his very presence on the pitch and the energy the opposition had to expend to keep him in check that made him so dangerous. Even the goals he didn't score in 1970 were brilliant, or at least required brilliance to stop them: a blast from inside his own half against Czechoslovakia that sailed just right of the post; a magnificent dummy sold to Uruguayan keeper Ladislao Mazurkiewicz, which he then collected and contrived to put wide; and the superb downward header that produced the 'Save of the Century' from England's Gordon Banks. Fittingly, Pelé opened the scoring in the final against Italy (Brazil's 100th World Cup goal, no less) and proved instrumental in one of the great team performances in history as the *Seleçao* dismantled the *Azzurri* 4–1.

'O Rei' retired from international football in July 1971, but continued playing for Santos and then the New York Cosmos until 1977. In retirement, Pelé has tried many vocations (to varying degrees of success), including UN ambassador, Brazilian politician, actor (in the classic *Escape to Victory*) and boner-pill salesman. He still retains God-like status in the game well into his seventies and, although his wonderful performances are now consigned to second-hand stories and grainy YouTube footage, the younger generation can still experience what it was like to see Pelé play: just ramp up that video game player to 100/100 and watch him tear the opposition apart.

Bobby Moore, England 1962, 1966, 1970

Quite often the best way to judge a man is to listen to what others say about him. That being the case, Bobby Moore was quite a footballer and quite a man. His England coach, Alf Ramsey, called him a footballer 'I could trust with my life', while opponents Franz Beckenbauer and Pelé said he was the best defender they had ever faced. But it is what Moore's contemporaries said about him as a man that really stood out, painting a picture of a down-to-earth leader with integrity, compassion and character; as true an English gentleman as you could hope to find on the football pitch.

As far as his talents were concerned, Moore was by no means exceptional. He didn't have blinding pace, was average in the air and played with an unorthodox, chest-out, upright style. But all this did not take into account the east Londoner's work ethic, footballing brain and impeccable sense of timing. As West Ham and England teammate Geoff Hurst once said:

> 66They said he couldn't run, but he was rarely beaten to the ball. They said that he couldn't jump, but he was rarely beaten in the air. He recognised that he was deficient in some areas and compensated by working hard on the training pitch and focusing on his positional play.99

Moore's rise to the top of the English game was meteoric: he made his debut for West Ham as a seventeen-year-old in 1958 and four years later he had progressed to such an extent that he was selected for the 1962 World Cup squad, where he played all four games in Chile. The following year he was handed the England captaincy, an honour he held for a decade. The twenty-five-year-old had already captained West Ham to FA Cup and European Cup Winners' Cup final wins by the time the World Cup rolled around in 1966, and expectations were high that Moore could lead his team to victory in the greatest international tournament too.

His influence on the home finals was immeasurable, leading by example and being the archetypal 'coach on the pitch' for boss Alf Ramsey. While Hurst and Charlton got the headlines, it was Moore who lifted the Jules Rimet trophy in front of an adoring home crowd. Images of that day are still rolled out every four years to give England fans hope the achievement can one day be matched.

Although 1966 was a career high point, Moore was actually at his peak in the 1970 tournament. After shrugging off a bogus shoplifting charge during a pre-tournament tour of Colombia, England's captain was at his imperious best against Brazil, turning back wave after wave of attacks with superior positioning and well-timed tackles; one such intervention, against the onrushing Jairzinho, is still held up as the greatest tackle in English football. Many say it was his greatest game in an England shirt. Moore's performance that day was not enough to avoid a 1–0 defeat, and he and his team came up short again in the quarterfinal against West Germany, seeing a 2–0 lead turn into a 3–2 extra-time defeat.

England's captain would play one more qualification campaign, but a 1–1 draw with Poland in the final game meant England didn't qualify for the finals in West Germany, and Moore made his record 108th and final appearance for the Three Lions against Italy in November 1973.

He later joined Fulham and played a couple of years in the USA in the North American Soccer League, but upon retirement from the game the coaching job he so coveted never materialised, despite reportedly agreeing to a deal with Elton John to be the boss of Watford in 1977. Instead he worked as a journalist and broadcaster before announcing he had been diagnosed with bowel and liver cancer in early February 1993. England's greatest-ever footballer passed away on 24 February 1993, and a nation mourned the loss of a true hero and a gentleman.

Eusébio, Portugal 1966

But for a chance conversation in a barbershop, the World Cup may never have been graced by one of its all-time greats, Portugal forward Eusébio. In 1960, Benfica coach Béla Guttmann was getting a haircut when he overheard a visiting coach from Sao Paolo mention a phenomenal player he had seen while touring in Mozambique and, after flying to the capital, Lourenço Marques (now Maputo), Guttman signed the eighteen-year-old from under the noses of rivals Sporting for £7500; within a fortnight, Eusébio was fast-tracked to be eligible to play for Portugal too.

The African teen became an instant success for both Benfica and his adopted country. In his second full season in Lisbon, he won the European Cup, scoring twice against the mighty Real Madrid in a scintillating 5–3 win, and came second in the Ballon d'Or voting. In total, Eusébio ended up winning eleven domestic titles with the *Águias*, as well as the Ballon d'Or in 1965 and three runners-up medals in the European Cup (1962–63, 1964–65 and 1967–68).

For Portugal, 'The Black Panther' was just as prolific, helping to guide them to their first-ever World Cup finals in 1966 with seven goals in qualifying. In England he was virtually unplayable, his speed and strength of shot causing defenders problems in every game he played, despite being the only player of real quality in the Portugal team (a situation with which Cristiano Ronaldo can empathise with the current national team).

Eusébio gave warning of his talents with two goals against Brazil in the final group game, but no-one was ready for what came next: trailing 3–0 to an upstart North Korea team in the quarterfinal, Eusébio went on a one-man tear that remains one of the greatest individual performances in World Cup history. By the time he had finished ripping the opposition to shreds with a ferocious performance, he'd scored four goals and turned a potential shock defeat into a comfortable 5–3 win.

Against the hosts in the semifinal his luck finally ran out; he scored from the penalty spot, but it proved merely a consolation as England progressed to the final 2–1. Eusébio left the Wembley pitch in a flood of tears that night, unaware of the fact that it was his last competitive game at the World Cup. (He scored a goal in the third-place playoff against the Soviet Union two days later to win the Golden Boot, but it's debatable as to how competitive those games were.) Finishing his career with forty-one goals in sixty-four internationals, Eusébio's talents alone could not help drag some pretty average Portugal sides to another World Cup, despite playing in the 1970 and 1974 qualifiers.

While he played his international football for Portugal, Eusébio has always considered himself an African footballer and is widely regarded as Africa's greatest player, blazing a trail for other African greats such as Roger Milla, Hossam Hassan, Finidi George and Didier Drogba to make their mark in the finals.

As for where he stands in the pantheon of Portuguese greats, especially with a certain Cristiano Ronaldo currently gaining all the headlines, Eusébio is in no doubt: 'Seven times best footballer [in Portugal], top scorer at the World Cup, voted into the all-time FIFA top ten — those are just the facts,' he said in an interview in 2010.

> **I'm not sure whether anyone can surpass that.
> It's up to [the press] to decide. I'm proud to say
> I've done something for the good of football.
> I don't compare myself to anyone.**

And so he shouldn't.

Sadly, 'The Black Panther' passed away on 5 January 2014, his old sparring partner Bobby Charlton leading the tributes by remembering him as 'one of the finest players I ever had the privilege to play against', while former Portugal captain Luis Figo simply called him 'the greatest'.

Franz Beckenbauer, West Germany 1966, 1970, 1974

Few men have achieved as much in the game as Franz *'Der Kaiser'* Beckenbauer. For Bayern Munich, he won five Bundesliga titles, four German Cups and three European Cups over thirteen years, while for West Germany he came first, second and third in the three tournaments he played in, redefining the role of the *libero* while he was at it. As a coach, he guided West Germany to the final in 1986 (where they lost to Argentina) and won the tournament in 1990, becoming the first player in history to win the World Cup as both a captain and coach.

He is also said to have invented lederhosen, to have designed the new Audi A5 on the back of a napkin and to hold the all-time record for stein drinking at the Löwenbräukeller in Munich (and if he didn't, then it was just because he was too busy doing other important stuff ...).

There were few who saw Beckenbauer play in the early years that doubted he would go on to achieve great things. He made his West Germany debut in September 1965 after just one full season in the Bayern side, and he already possessed the graceful technique and flawless distribution he would soon become renowned for. His performances with his club side won him a place in the 1966 World Cup team aged just twenty, where he announced his arrival with two goals in the opening group game against Switzerland. Playing in midfield, Beckenbauer pulled the strings for the German team and he scored the winner in the semifinal against Russia. In the final he was given the task of man-marking England star Bobby Charlton, which stifled his own attacking drive and is often cited as why West Germany lost the game. 'England beat us in 1966 because Bobby Charlton was just a little bit better than me,' he later admitted, although having his vision impaired by Charlton's windswept comb-over must have been a factor too.

Despite starting to experiment by playing in a more deep-lying playmaker role for Bayern, Beckenbauer remained in the West German midfield for Mexico 70, where he was in majestic form and led his country to the semifinal. Along the way, he gained a measure of revenge against England in the quarterfinal, exploiting the freedom afforded him when Bobby Charlton was subbed off to lead West Germany back from 2–0 down to win 3–2. In an epic 4–3 semifinal loss to Italy, Beckenbauer played much of the second half with a dislocated shoulder and, despite having his arm strapped to his side in a makeshift sling, he still looked the classiest player on the pitch.

By 1974 Beckenbauer had perfected the *libero* role — that of a deep-lying playmaker who would bring the ball out of defence and begin attacks — and it was from this new position that he led West Germany to the pinnacle of the game on home soil. A loss to East Germany was the only blot on their copybook as they reached the final against favourites the Netherlands, Beckenbauer exerting more and more influence both on and off the pitch as the tournament progressed.

The Netherlands' style of Total Football made them the darlings of the world game, and when they went 1–0 up within a minute an *Oranje* victory looked inevitable. But the Netherlands preferred to showboat rather than kill the game off and, with Beckenbauer finding his feet, the West Germans got back into the game, first equalising through a Paul Breitner penalty and then taking the lead through Gerd Müller just before half-time. As Beckenbauer later noted:

> **Going a goal down was good for us. The Dutch eased off and we were able to get into the match. And once you've relaxed your grip, it's hard to recover the initiative.**

Despite their spirited efforts, the Netherlands couldn't find a way through West Germany's defence in the second half and Beckenbauer became the first captain to raise the new World Cup trophy aloft in front of his hometown fans in the Olympiastadion.

'*Der Kaiser*' would go on to play another three years for West Germany, retiring from international football with 103 caps, before heading off to the US to play with Pelé at the New York Cosmos. However, there was another chapter in Beckenbauer's World Cup career to be written; despite not having any of the relevant badges or previous coaching experience, he guided his country to two consecutive finals (1986 and 1990), winning against Argentina in Italia 90. That victory holds a special place in Beckenbauer's heart: 'I would say 1990 was the most important to me. It doesn't come any better than managing a side to victory.'

Beckenbauer delivered a third World Cup to Germany in his role as chairman of the Germany 2006 World Cup Organising Committee, and as an ex-FIFA executive he is still actively involved in the administration of the game. Unfortunately, that frequently means being a lapdog for FIFA president Sepp Blatter, toeing the party line rather than freely expressing himself, as he did so gracefully on the pitch. Responding to reports of slave labour being used in Qatar to build World Cup infrastructure, Beckenbauer said:

> **I have not seen a single slave in Qatar. I don't know where these reports come from. I've been to Qatar and have a completely different picture of it. I think mine is more realistic.**

Because the all-expenses paid, first-class flying, chauffeur-driven mode of visiting a country is the best way to expose modern-day slavery, eh Frankie?

Gerd Müller, West Germany 1970, 1974

Gerd Müller may have lost his all-time goalscoring record to Brazil's Ronaldo in 2006, but the West German remains the World Cup's pre-eminent goalscorer. His stocky frame, lightning reactions and killer instinct made him the ultimate poacher, and whether it was for club (365 Bundesliga goals for Bayern Munich) or country (sixty-eight in sixty-two), he had an uncanny knack for being in the right place at the right time.

Scoring fourteen goals in just thirteen World Cup matches, *'Der Bomber'* also did his best work in the biggest of games: he grabbed the extra-time winner in the 1970 quarterfinal against England, scored twice in the semifinal loss against Italy in the next game, and got the winner against the Netherlands four years later to win the World Cup Final. Simply put, if you had to bet your life savings on a player scoring from one chance in a World Cup game, you'd take Gerd Müller every time.

Making his debut for West Germany soon after the 1966 tournament, in the four years between finals he forged a reputation as one of the most feared strikers in football at Bayern Munich. In 1970, his first foray into the finals, Müller proved a revelation, teaming up with Uwe Seeler to form the most potent front line in the tournament. He scored seven goals in the first three group games and followed it up with a crucial winner against old enemy England in the quarterfinal; by the time West Germany were knocked out in the semifinal, Müller had found the net an incredible ten times and won the Golden Boot.

While less prolific four years later on home soil, the twenty-eight-year-old was at the peak of his game, replacing quantity with quality when it came to goals. His 76th-minute strike against

Poland in the last game of the second group stage sent West Germany to the final, where he scored the winning goal against the Netherlands with a typical opportunist's strike. No goal better summed up Müller in the World Cup; a short, sharp run into space in the box to receive the ball, followed by a quick back-pedal and snap shot, highlighted the full array of the man's talents.

It was the perfect final goal to sign off a World Cup career with. Müller announced his retirement after the victorious final; aged just twenty-eight, one could only imagine how far he could have stretched his record goalscoring tally if he had played in Argentina too.

Müller endured a tough time after retirement from football, struggling with alcoholism and, if not for the help of former teammate and Bayern president Uli Hoeness, he may have descended too far to return.

'Uli saved my life,' said Müller. 'I couldn't have coped on my own.' Hoeness gave him a job as assistant manager for Bayern Munich's reserve team in 1992, where he still remains today.

Records are made to be broken, but nowhere is judging the best by where they are placed on an all-time list more flawed than with the World Cup goalscorers. Brazil's Ronaldo required another tournament (six more games) to break Müller's record, and compatriot Miroslav Klose, who joined him on fourteen goals after the 2010 tournament, scored half of his total against Saudi Arabia, Costa Rica and Ecuador.

Gerd Müller is the World Cup's greatest striker, and don't let anyone tell you differently.

Johan Cruyff, the Netherlands 1974

It's extremely difficult to overstate the influence of Johan Cruyff, a footballing figure of such otherworldly skill and visionary thinking that his impact on the game is still being felt today. Despite playing in only one World Cup tournament and making just forty-eight appearances for his country, few players can lay claim to having more effect on the modern game than the Netherlands' legendary No.14.

Dutch football history is divided into two eras: before and after Cruyff. Up to the point where the nineteen-year-old Amsterdam native made his debut against Hungary in September 1966, the Netherlands had appeared in just two World Cup finals (1934 and 1938), making little impact on the footballing world. After Cruyff, the game would never be the same again, in the Netherlands or anywhere else.

Together with legendary coach Rinus Michels, Cruyff created Total Football, a possession/pressing style that saw players constantly shifting positions on the field; as the master playmaker, provider and goalscorer, Cruyff would roam the field, constantly probing to find his most effective position, while his teammates filled in the other roles around him. Total Football had already worked to devastating effect at club level with Ajax, leading to eight Eredivisie titles and three consecutive European Cups from 1971 to 1973, so when Michels took control of the national team for the 1974 World Cup the Netherlands were quickly installed as one of the favourites to lift the trophy.

An obdurate man at the best of times, Cruyff made waves both on and off the pitch in West Germany. Before a ball had been kicked, he informed Netherlands officials he would not be wearing the three-striped kit of sponsor adidas, as he had a contract with Puma — so a special 'two-stripe' kit was created just for him. It was the smallest of compromises considering Cruyff's place in the team, but it did speak to a stubborn 'it's my way or the wrong way' attitude that was a constant in his career.

Things couldn't have been smoother on the pitch, though, as the Netherlands cruised through their qualifying group. Wins over Uruguay and Bulgaria might have showcased the Netherlands' best football, but it was a nondescript 0–0 draw with Sweden that will go down in history for being the first time the 'Cruyff turn' was executed in a game, the Dutch master faking one way and then dragging the ball behind him with his instep to completely bamboozle Jan Olsson. (Don't worry, Jan — you might have been the first but you weren't the last to be beaten by that brilliant move.)

It was in the second group stage that Cruyff's team really made people sit up and take notice, challenging the established order of the World Cup by breaking the stranglehold of the traditional powers. The Netherlands destroyed Argentina 4–0 with a wonderful display of attacking football before turning national stereotypes on their head in the game against Brazil, where it was Brazil that was cast in the role of the traditional 'European bully', unable to live with the craft and guile of the fluid Dutch; Cruyff's volley for the Netherlands' second was a goal Garrincha or Pelé would've been proud of.

Heavily favoured in the final against West Germany, Total Football reached its pinnacle in the first minute of the game, the Netherlands passing between themselves from the kick-off until Cruyff turned on the pace and won a penalty. The Netherlands were 1–0 up and Germany hadn't touched the ball. Unfortunately, the Netherlands were so intent on dominating their opponent, they forgot the small matter of getting more goals (they 'forgot to score a second', as winger Johnny Rep would later admit); a resolute West German side scored twice before the half, and repelled all the Netherlands could throw at them in the second half, to emerge 2–1 winners. The result shocked the world and although Cruyff would later say, 'There is no better medal than being acclaimed for your style', the game is still known as 'The Lost Final' to the Dutch.

(Cruyff was strangely subdued during the final, and some have attested his performance to a story published on the eve of the game by German tabloid *Bild-Zeitung* entitled 'Cruyff, champagne, naked girls and a cool bath' that revealed the Netherlands' penchant for partying a little too hard. While the players called it a newspaper stitch-up, Cruyff was said to have spent the entire night before the final on the phone to his wife, Danny, trying to extricate himself from the doghouse.)

West Germany 74 proved to be Cruyff's last appearance at a World Cup. Despite playing for the Netherlands throughout the qualifiers for the 1978 edition, he decided not to travel to Argentina after a failed kidnapping attempt on his family in Barcelona the year before. However, the Dutchman continued to have a massive impact on the game for decades after, due to the coaching philosophy he instilled at Ajax and Barcelona. Ajax's 'football factory' produced the majority of the Dutch team that won Euro 92 and made the quarterfinals in 1994, and as coach of Barça's 'Dream Team' he worked with a virtual who's who of World Cup heroes, including Gheorghe Hagi, Romário, Hristo Stoichkov, Michael Laudrup and Ronald Koeman, as well as giving future Barcelona coach Pep Guardiola his debut as a player.

Cruyff's coaching ideology remains strong to the present day, and his influence can be seen in Spain's all-conquering national team, the Barcelona side of the last decade, and now with Bayern Munich under Guardiola. Not a bad legacy for a bloke with just seven World Cup games to his name, eh?

Diego Maradona, Argentina 1982, 1986, 1990, 1994

Now for the story of a man who was literally dragged from a shit-hole in Buenos Aires and reached the pinnacle of world football. Diego Maradona's journey to becoming the greatest footballer to ever play the game (sorry, Pelé) is as engrossing a narrative as you will find in life, let alone sport. Born with prodigious footballing talent in a ghetto in the Argentinean capital, El Diego was taken from a life of poverty to one of God-like adulation and hedonistic excess that ultimately proved his downfall. That the rise and fall of Diego Maradona took place almost entirely at the World Cup only serves to make his tale more captivating.

As far as 'rags to riches' stories go, being pulled out of the shit as a youngster is a pretty good one. A young Diego was saved by his uncle from drowning in the family cesspit, and the story has been used frequently to highlight Maradona's flight from the poverty of his Villa Fiorito birthplace. Said to have honed his ball skills by playing with an orange in the street, he soon became a footballing phenom, schooling kids twice his size in impromptu street games and wowing the crowds with displays of his ball skills during halftime at local matches.

Maradona had his first trial when he was just nine (he was so good, the coach thought he was a midget) and made his senior debut for Argentinos Juniors at fifteen; a year later he had played his first game for the national team, against Hungary. However, Maradona was to suffer his first footballing disappointment when César Luis Menotti deemed him too young to compete in the 1978 finals and he had to watch from the sidelines as the *albiceleste* won the World Cup on home soil.

As he'd agreed to join Barcelona at the conclusion of the tournament, Spanish crowds were eager to see Maradona in action in España 82 — but the weight of expectation proved too much for the twenty-one-year-old. Rumours of the stocky young South American who could take games over with his wand of a left foot had reached European shores, and teams adapted their tactics accordingly. In the second round 'Group of Death' featuring Italy and Brazil, Maradona was a marked man. Italian Claudio Gentile was given the job of man-marking Diego in the first game, and proceeded to prod, shove, and kick him at every opportunity.

'In the whole game, he tried to steal the ball one or two times, the rest of the time he dedicated to kicking me,' said Maradona; the stats backed him up, with Gentile committing twenty-three fouls (and shown just a yellow card) for his day's work. Against Brazil, he was given just as much attention from the *Seleçao* defenders and, as Argentina's World Cup defence slipped away with a 3–1 defeat, Maradona lunged at one of his tormentors and was sent off in the dying minutes.

El Diego lost the trust of his countrymen after his red card, and he didn't play a game for Argentina in more than two years. Coach Carlos Bilardo kept the faith though, regularly visiting Maradona in Napoli and responding to critics by predicting he would be the best player in the 1986 World Cup.

Maradona was named captain of his country (controversially ahead of national treasure Daniel Passarella) and repaid Bilardo's faith by stamping his name all over the tournament. It would be doing his teammates a disservice to say Maradona single-handedly won the 1986 World Cup, but Maradona *did* single-handedly win the 1986 World Cup. For opposing teams, it was a case of pick your poison: stand off him and he would beat you with a killer pass; play him close and he would breeze past you with speed and strength; foul him and face the wrath of his dead ball skills. All those attributes — as well as what *L'Equipe* called his 'half angel, half devil' personality — were on show against England in the highly charged quarterfinal in Mexico City. His first goal was all devilry, a cheeky hand extended as he jumped for a high ball with Peter Shilton; his second, a breathtaking run from halfway through the England defence that is viewed as the greatest goal ever scored.

Proving his ability to take control of games was no flash in the pan, Maradona did it again against Belgium in the semifinal, scoring two breathtaking individual goals.

'Without Diego, we would not have won with such brilliancy,' said teammate Jorge Valdano. 'Those goals raised football to a higher level and confirmed his condition as a football artist.'

In the final against West Germany he was kept relatively quiet by the limpet-like attentions of Lothar Matthäus, but he still had a hand in all three goals, including unlocking the German defence with an instinctive pass that sent Jorge Burruchaga away to score the winner with only two minutes to go. Maradona had led his team to a World Cup win and confirmed his place as the world's greatest player; the pictures of the joyous Argentina captain being carried on the shoulders of his teammates around the Azteca pitch live long in the memory.

The late '80s saw Maradona reach both the peak of the game and the height of his popularity. He won two Serie A titles with Napoli (1986–87 and 1989–90) and dragged an average Argentina side to another World Cup Final in 1990, despite playing with the pain of knee and ankle injuries from years of being a magnet to barely legal tackles and challenges. But his highs in Italy weren't just confined to achievements on the pitch, as he developed an addiction to cocaine and fell under the influence of the local Neapolitan mafia. Stories of his womanising and drug-fuelled binges did the rounds, adding to his bad-boy legend, until he failed a drug test after a game against Bari in 1991 and was handed a fifteen-month ban from football.

Seemingly on the road to recovery following stints at Seville and Newell's Old Boys, Diego returned to the national team to help them qualify for the 1994 finals. In the US, he showed flashes of the old Maradona in the two games he played, even scoring against Greece. His maniacal face-in-the-camera celebration was laughed off as 'Diego being Diego' — with some even suggesting he might inspire Argentina to a third consecutive trip to the final — until it was announced he had failed a drug test for the stimulant ephedrine and was unceremoniously thrown out of the tournament. The expulsion led to the end of his international career and, after failing a third drug test while playing for Boca Juniors in 1997, he called time on club football too.

The following years saw Maradona find newer and more dangerous ways to ruin his life, the lowlights including a massive weight gain, a three-year suspended sentence for firing a rifle at a group of journalists and a drug-induced heart attack. There were real fears for his life at one point, but the El Diego roller-coaster got back on track when a svelte, seemingly reborn Maradona was announced as Argentina manager in 2008.

Unfortunately his strange selection policy and tactical naivety as a coach saw the *albiceleste* barely qualify for South Africa 2010, where they were humiliated by Germany in the quarterfinals. After the defeat, forced out by those who hired him, he let rip in typical fashion.

'[National team general manager] Bilardo lied to me,' said Maradona. 'While we were in mourning [at the World Cup exit], he was working in the shadows to have us thrown out.'

Reconciling Maradona the footballer and Maradona the man can be a difficult undertaking. Some choose to ignore it completely — FIFA's official profile on him makes no mention of the 1994 finals at all, let alone the drug test that ended his World Cup career — while others use his transgressions to elevate Pelé above him as the greatest ever. (Maradona has countered this by saying FIFA's award to Pelé as their best-ever player 'isn't worth a dick'.) Whatever your opinion of Diego Maradona, whether you think he was a footballing deity or just an extraordinary mortal, when he was out on the pitch there was no denying he was God's gift to football.

Ronaldo, Brazil 1994, 1998, 2002, 2006

Should Ronaldo be considered Brazil's greatest-ever player? As sacrilegious as this statement first sounds, a look at the man they called '*O Fenômeno*'s CV shows that he should at least be sitting on the arm of Pelé's throne, if not sliding down to squeeze in beside him: a double World Cup winner, two-time World Player of the Year, all-time leading World Cup goalscorer and, as a highly publicised scandal with three cross-dressing prostitutes would corroborate, no problems with erectile dysfunction (unlike Pelé, with his later life admissions while selling little blue pills).

Discovered by 1970 World Cup legend Jairzinho, Ronaldo Luís Nazário de Lima burst onto the scene with Cruzeiro in 1993, his powerful physique and clinical finishing earning him a spot in Brazil's 1994 World Cup squad. But unlike Pelé, who had a massive impact on the 1958 tournament as a seventeen-year-old, Ronaldo had to be content with a permanent place on the bench, learning his apprenticeship from Romário and Bebeto as Brazil won their fourth world title.

Ronaldo went about building his legend in European football, dominating the Dutch, Spanish and Italian leagues in quick succession thanks to stints at PSV, Barcelona and Inter Milan. His balance, strength and eye for goal certainly made him deserving of the '*O Fenômeno*' — 'The Phenomenon' — nickname, and the plaudits quickly followed: he won the World Footballer of the Year award in 1996 and 1997, the youngest to do so and the first to win it back to back.

When the 1998 World Cup kicked off in France, the twenty-one-year-old was undeniably the world's best footballer — and he went about backing that up with four goals en route to the final. But on the day football's young king was to be coronated, an ill and dazed Ronaldo staggered through the 3–0 loss to France, clearly still feeling the effects of an earlier fit he'd suffered in the team hotel (see Chapter 9 for more details). The previously invincible Brazilian suddenly looked fallible, and it was just the first in a series of injuries and setbacks that blighted the rest of his career.

In November 1999 he suffered a serious knee injury against Lecce that required surgery, and he lasted just seven minutes in his comeback match against Lazio five months later before his leg gave way again. Ronaldo missed the entire 2000–01 season and there were real fears that his career could be over but, after fifteen months out of the game, he made a dramatic comeback and earned a place in the 2002 World Cup squad. In Japan/Korea, Ronaldo was reborn; combining magnificently with strike partner Rivaldo, he scored eight goals in the tournament, including both in the final against Germany, despite having the weight of the world's worst haircut on his head. To top it off, he won his third World Player of the Year award.

A move to Real Madrid in 2002 saw him join the ranks of the Galácticos, where he enjoyed life to the full — both on and off the pitch, as his growing waistline highlighted. The added girth didn't stop the goals coming, though, as he scored twenty-three in his first title-winning season. But injuries soon reared their head again, and he spent a considerable amount of time on the treatment table. Again, the World Cup provided him with a chance for redemption, and in 2006 he broke Gerd Müller's thirty-two-year-old all-time goalscoring record, striking twice against Japan to tie with the German, and then finding the net against Ghana in the Round of 16 to own the record outright. Although Brazil exited the finals against France in the quarterfinal, Ronaldo had secured his place in World Cup history, overcoming a fair amount of adversity along the way.

A third knee injury while playing for AC Milan in 2008 saw another lengthy rehab period, before he enjoyed a mini-revival at Corinthians, winning the Campeonato Paulista and the Brazilian Cup in 2009, before finally announcing his retirement from the game in 2011.

And so, back to the question: should Ronaldo be considered Brazil's greatest-ever player? While 'O Fenômeno' will never be considered Pelé's equal — 'O Rei' will never be touched in that regard — the sheer weight of Ronaldo's silverware means he proudly occupies second place, alongside Garrincha and Leônidas.

Zinedine Zidane, France 1998, 2002, 2006

Until the night of 9 July 2006, the exclusive club of 'World Cup geniuses who are also complete nutjobs' had just one member: Diego Maradona. Then France's Zinedine Zidane launched himself headfirst into the chest of Italy's Marco Materazzi during the second period of extra time and El Diego suddenly had to rush to the ink-jet printer to make up another homemade membership card. Zidane's moment of madness has, for many, come to define him, obscuring a sparkling career that saw him win the World Cup in 1998 and take home the World Player of the Year award on no less than three occasions (1998, 2000 and 2003).

Brought up in a tough neighbourhood of Marseille, Zidane learnt his football — as well as his values — on the streets, and both were heavily influenced by that environment. Zizou's football was all about the deft touches, body swerves and calmness under pressure that only street football can teach, but he also developed an 'eye-for-an-eye' attitude when it came to being fouled or provoked.

'You'll get knocks from now until the end of your career,' Cannes coach Guy Lacombe warned Zidane, rather presciently, when he started with the youth team.

> **That's just how it is for players as gifted as you. If you take the law into your own hands, you'll spend your life on the sidelines watching everyone else play.**

Making his France debut in 1994 while still at Bordeaux, he had to wait until the 1998 finals to finally show his talents on the world stage. Perhaps overcome by the pressure and expectations of a home finals, Zizou struggled in the opening round and was sent off for stamping on an opponent in the game against Saudi Arabia. Making up for lost time after a two-game suspension, Zidane promptly guided France to the final against Brazil, where his two headed goals set *Les Bleus* up for a 3–0 win. Recalling his days back on the streets of Marseille, Zidane said after the win:

> **Like all children, in our neighbourhood we played our own World Cups. When I ended up taking part in one for real, I always remembered that — the times me and my neighbourhood friends had played in our own little World Cup. In a way, I was representing them.**

Feted as a national hero, Zidane went on to further success with club and country, winning titles with Juventus and then Real Madrid, as well as winning Euro 2000 with France. With arguably a better team as defending champions in 2002, France were rocked by an thigh injury to Zidane just before the tournament and the two games he missed saw France lose both without scoring a goal; his appearance in the final game against Denmark smacked of desperation and a 2–0 defeat sent France out of the World Cup goalless, the worst performance by a defending champion in the history of the tournament.

An opportunity for redemption arrived in 2006, when Zidane came out of international retirement to get the band together one last time. With fellow 1998 winners Lilian Thùram, Patrick Vieira and Thierry Henry along for the ride, Zidane was in sparkling form throughout, destroying Brazil in the quarterfinal and scoring the winner from the spot in the semi against Portugal.

In the final against Italy his cheeky chipped penalty gave France the lead but, with Italy scoring before the half, the score remained tied as the match went to extra time and towards penalties. Then came Zidane's head-butt and red card, fulfilling the words of coach Lacombe more than a decade before; he took the law into his own hands and paid a heavy price, as France went on to lose the final in the subsequent shootout.

Despite apologising to his teammates for what happened, Zidane was unrepentant after the match. For Zizou, the code of the street proved stronger than the laws of the game as one of the brightest World Cup stars signed off in the most shocking of circumstances.

- 5 -

WORLD CUP SUPERSTARS AND CULT HEROES

The allure of the World Cup isn't solely down to the men at the very top of the footballing totem pole. Players such as Pelé, Diego Maradona, Bobby Moore and Franz Beckenbauer deserve to be recognised as the bona fide legends of the game, but the tournament is so much more than its greatest practitioners.

What makes the World Cup so compelling is that, very often, you don't know where the next superstar is going to come from. This book's superstars take many guises, from France's mercurial Michel Platini, who captained his country in some of the tournament's most exciting games but couldn't lead them to a final, to Germany captain Fritz Walter, who inspired his country to victory in the 1954 final against the hitherto invincible Hungary. They have enjoyed a sustained period of success (Brazil's Garrincha, who won consecutive finals in '58 and '62) and made an incredible impact on just one tournament (Eusébio in 1966). One sealed his legend with his countrymen by scoring a last-minute winner in the final (Andrés Iniesta in 2010) while others have appeared out of nowhere, only to disappear just as fast (Italy's Golden Boot winner 'Totò' Schillaci and five-goals-in-a-game record holder Oleg Salenko).

And then there are the cult heroes, those who take their place in the annals of World Cup history for a flash of genius or momentary brain-snap of madness. These men are slightly harder to define: one made himself a laughing-stock of world football by ignoring the rules of the game, while another came from a country (Azerbaijan) that has never played in the finals.

But special mention must be made of Pickles, the greatest World Cup cult hero of all time, who was never so much as within a sniff of a tournament match (but then that's most likely due to the fact that he was a dog).

José Nasazzi, Uruguay 1930

Uruguay's captain and greatest-ever player, José Nasazzi was already a legend by the time the first World Cup kicked off in his homeland, having guided his country to two Olympic golds (1924 and 1928) and three Copa Americas (1923, 1924 and 1926). Born in 1901 in Montevideo to Italian and Spanish parents, Nasazzi began his playing career with Lito as a seventeen-year-old, but enjoyed his best days at Bella Vista where he played a decade at right-back.

In an era when the coach was not as influential as he was to later become, Nasazzi was Uruguay's leader, barking orders on the pitch and deciding tactics and team selection off it. His voice was the one the Uruguayan players listened to the most — he was nicknamed '*El Gran Mariscal*' ('The Great Marshall') — and he was said to have made a particularly rousing speech at half-time during the final when *La Celeste* trailed Argentina 2–1.

Nasazzi was a tough, uncompromising character who led by example and expected nothing but complete effort from his teammates. His crowning moment came in leading his country to a historic 4–2 come-from-behind victory over rivals Argentina in the first World Cup Final, although he wasn't actually handed the trophy in the traditional manner at the end of the game — that honour went to Dr Raul Jude of the Uruguayan Football Federation (FIFA looking after the suits as usual). Over a fourteen-year national team career, he won relatively few caps — forty-one — but there's no denying that with seven major trophies to his name (he added another Copa America in 1935) he made each and every one count.

Fritz Walter, Germany 1954, 1958

Germans of a certain age still call a miserable, rainy day 'Fritz Walter weather' in honour of their inspirational and much-loved former captain who played his best football in wet, torrid conditions. So when a thirty-three-year-old Walter looked out of his hotel window on the morning of the 1954 World Cup Final to see dark clouds forming over the city of Bern, he must have had a wry smile on his face. If the weather took a turn for the worse, maybe there was a chance West Germany could beat the highly fancied Magical Magyars of Hungary. It proved to be an omen, as Walter inspired his country to a shock 3–2 win in the Wankdorf Stadium (no reason to mention the stadium other than it's great to write the word 'Wankdorf').

Fritz Walter was the archetypal hometown hero, playing his entire career in the town of his birth, Kaiserslautern, where he appeared more than 400 times between 1939 and 1959. His almost two-decade-long international career began in 1940 (he scored a hat-trick against Romania) but, due to WWII and a four-year ban by FIFA, West Germany did not resume internationals until 1950, by which time Walter had moved from centre forward into a deeper, more influential role.

In the 1954 finals, no-one gave West Germany a snowball's chance in hell of winning, especially when they were beaten 8–3 by Hungary in the group stages. But the Germans battled on, beating Yugoslavia and the highly rated Austrian team 6–1 in the semifinal. It was in the semi that Walter was at his commanding best, pulling the strings in a forceful performance that saw him score twice and set up two more. In the final four days later, Walter rallied his side from 2–0 down and helped them take full advantage of the few opportunities they were offered by Hungary. With just six minutes remaining, Walter's half-cleared cross fell to Helmut Rahn to knock in the winner.

Walter helped restore some pride to West Germany with the World Cup win, and he went on to become the most popular footballer in his country's history; the German Football Federation voted him their most outstanding talent of the previous fifty years in a UEFA poll in 2004. He helped his country make the semifinal in 1958 but, at age thirty-seven, his influence was on the wane and they lost 3–1 to hosts Sweden.

In retirement, Walter returned home — 1. FC Kaiserslautern re-named their Betzenberg Stadium in his honour in 1985 — where he ran a couple of businesses with his wife, Italia, until his death in 2002.

Garrincha, Brazil 1958, 1962, 1966

The man known as 'The Little Bird' shouldn't even have been able to play football, let alone be considered one of Brazil's greatest-ever players. A childhood sickness left Manuel Francisco dos Santos — 'Garrincha' to everyone but his mum — with one leg longer than the other, and both of them bowed like John Wayne's after a ride through Monument Valley.

But what he lacked aesthetically he more than made up for on the pitch. He was a mesmerising lightning-bolt of a player who could make the ball bend — quite literally in the case of his free kicks — to his will. Garrincha was the ultimate footballing nonconformist, often playing in a manner that was purely individualistic, with no regard for the goals of the team. He was called 'the most amateur footballer professional football has ever seen' by biographer Ruy Castro due to his often-insouciant attitude on the pitch and his reckless pursuit of the fast life off it.

Garrincha's first World Cup appearance came in the third game of the 1958 tournament, against the USSR, starting the game together with a teenage sensation called Pelé when calls for the dynamic duo to start could no longer be ignored (although Costa later revealed that Garrincha's omission from the first two group games was for tactical reasons). Their impact was immediate; French journalist Gabriel Hanot called the opening 180 seconds against the Russians the greatest three minutes in the history of football, as Garrincha ran rings around his hapless opponents and Brazil hit the woodwork twice before Vavá scored. Alongside established stars Mário Zagallo and the aforementioned Vavá, Pelé and Garrincha formed a near-unstoppable attacking force. In the final against Sweden, 'The Little Bird' set up two goals and commanded plenty of attention from the opponent's defence, allowing teammates to roam with impunity during the 5–2 win.

In 1962, Garrincha was the World Cup's undoubted star, especially after Brazil lost Pelé to injury in the second game. He was the dominant force in almost every contest, scoring twice against England and Chile en route to the final, and not even a controversial sending off in the semifinal — reversed on appeal — could stop him from winning his second consecutive world title.

As the player of the 1962 tournament, Garrincha was now a bona fide superstar and he lived the life of one, enjoying the company of more than a few beautiful ladies over the years. His World Cup story came to an end in disappointment in 1966 as an out-of-sorts Brazil were knocked out in the group stages — his final match against Hungary marked the first time in sixty games that Brazil had lost with Garrincha in the starting line-up.

Eventually, Garrincha's off-field lifestyle caught up with him. He enjoyed a drink as much as he enjoyed the ladies, and oftentimes combined the two to devastating effect. (Some reports have him fathering as many as fourteen children, although seven is said to be the more accurate figure.) His life gradually unravelled in a series of car crashes and domestic violence accusations before he passed away, aged just forty-nine, of cirrhosis of the liver in 1983. Brazil mourned a true hero, preferring to remember his achievements on the pitch rather than the transgressions off it.

Bobby Charlton, England 1958, 1962, 1966, 1970

It can be hard to recall what a truly brilliant footballer Bobby Charlton was in his day now that he's the septuagenarian ambassador for Manchester United who's rolled out every time the English tabloids need a quote about anything regarding Wayne Rooney or the England team. With his comb-over swaying this way and that, his turn of pace and ferocious shot made him a constant goal-scoring danger from deep, and it's no accident that both United and England reached the summit of the game while he was playing for them.

Charlton went to the World Cup in 1958 but didn't get the opportunity to take the field, due in some part to convalescing after being pulled from the wreckage of the Manchester United team plane that crashed on a Munich runway in the February of that year. Four years later, in Chile, Bobby got his chance. Playing out on the left, he scored his first World Cup goal against Argentina before suffering defeat to eventual winners Brazil in the quarterfinals.

In 1966, all the stars were aligned: England were hosting the World Cup, they were favourites to win the title and Charlton himself was at the height of his powers. He was the focal point of the England team and was quick to lay down a marker of things to come; his goal against Mexico in the second group game, where he ran from the halfway line before lashing the ball into the back of the net, is still considered one of his country's best.

Charlton's standout performances continued, with the only man playing to the same level being Portugal's dynamic forward Eusébio. When the two came head to head in the semifinal, it wasn't even a contest. The England midfielder had arguably his best game for the national team, scoring twice to lead his country to their first World Cup Final. The only downside of such a stellar outing was that fellow finalists Germany decided to man-mark Charlton with Franz Beckenbauer in the decider, effectively neutralising the two best talents on the pitch. Personal glory might have been something the humble Charlton never craved, but he got it anyway, celebrating England's 4–2 win as both the tournament's best player and European Footballer of the Year.

The 1970 finals in Mexico ended in bitter disappointment for Charlton. Cruising at 2–0 against West Germany in the quarterfinal, the midfielder was substituted in anticipation of the tough semifinal to come. Clearly England coach Alf Ramsey had underestimated Charlton's influence on the game; in his absence, Beckenbauer was able to take control of proceedings and lead his side on a dramatic comeback to win 3–2 in extra time. It was to be the last time Charlton played for England, an ignominious ending to an illustrious career.

Charlton played another two years for Manchester United before joining Preston North End as player-manager for a season in 1973–74, but coaching wasn't his calling and he moved into the world of business, setting up a series of successful football academies (one of which a young David Beckham attended, and was photographed receiving a prize from Charlton).

Now on the board of directors at Old Trafford, Charlton is held in the highest regard by the English footballing community — even more so after getting rid of his ridiculous comb-over.

Pickles the Dog, 1966

Sitting proudly with Lassie, Inspector Rex and the Littlest Hobo on the 'Dog Mount Rushmore', Pickles is bestowed World Cup cult hero status as the canine who helped recover the stolen Jules Rimet trophy in 1966. The trophy was nicked, to use English parlance, on 20 March from an event called the Stanley Gibbons 'Stampex' exhibition, despite the FA being given assurances that the trophy would be heavily guarded for the duration of its stay. (And who's scared of a bunch of stamp collectors anyway?)

A ransom call was made and the thief demanded £15,000 for the trophy's safe return. A meeting was arranged, fake notes were handed over and a bloke called Ted Betchley was arrested. Betchley eventually served two years for his part in the robbery, but at the time of his arrest he referred to a shadowy figured called 'The Pole' and refused to divulge where the trophy was.

On 27 March, Londoner David Corbett took his dog, Pickles, out for a walk in Beulah Hill, South London. When the mutt started snuffling around in a holly hedge, Corbett found an object wrapped in newspaper. Inside the ratty package was the Jules Rimet Trophy — Pickles had saved the day! Corbett was paid £5000 in reward — five times the amount the England players were paid for winning the final a couple of months later — and bought a house with the cash. Pickles became an overnight sensation, and for his find was given a medal by the National Canine Defence League and a year's supply of treats by a pet food company.

Asked about what it was like finding the trophy, Pickles said: 'Woof, woof, woof, growl', which is understandable seeing as dogs can't speak. The narrative of unearthing the trophy is probably better left to Corbett:

> **Even when I started taking off the paper and saw it was a statue, nothing really stirred. Then I noticed it said Brazil, West Germany and so on and I ran in to my wife immediately. It wasn't very World Cup-y though … very small.**

Unfortunately the story doesn't end happily. Firstly, Corbett's new adjective, 'World Cup-y', never really caught the imagination of the English public (no matter how many times he said: 'Okay love, I'm feeling a bit World Cup-y so I'm off to the pub to watch the match') and then, tragically, Pickles took the trip to the big kennel in the sky after hanging himself on his own lead in pursuit of a cat in August 1971.

Pak Doo-Ik, North Korea 1966

On the morning of 20 July 1966, the most famous footballer in the world wasn't Pelé, Bobby Charlton or Eusébio — he was a worker from a North Korean textbook factory called Pak Doo-Ik. The previous day, in front of nearly 18,000 raucous Ayresome Park fans, Doo-Ik scored the goal that would knock Italy out of the World Cup finals and send shockwaves through international football.

While the goal ensured his place in World Cup folklore, it also gave Doo-Ik and his North Korean teammates cult status with their North East hosts. The town of Middlesbrough took the players from the mysterious Asian nation to their heart — thousands of factory workers watched them train at the ICI chemical facility near town — and when Doo-Ik's goal went in, BBC commentator Frank Bough noted: 'They never cheer Middlesbrough like this.' The team became so well loved that 3000 Teesiders travelled by bus to Liverpool to watch North Korea's quarterfinal against Portugal.

While the Italians were greeted at home with a barrage of rotten fruit, the Koreans were rumoured to have been sent to prison for womanising and drinking in celebration of their World Cup achievements — although the players denied the jail time ever happened (but not the womanising and drinking, interestingly enough). Doo-Ik left the military and became a gymnastics teacher, even returning to Middlesbrough in 2002 as a guest of filmmaker Daniel Gordon, who made the documentary *The Game of Their Lives* about the team's 1966 exploits.

'The English people took us to their hearts and vice versa,' said Doo-Ik. 'I learnt that football is not about winning. Wherever we go ... playing football can improve diplomatic relations and promote peace.'

Pak Doo-Ik's moment in the sun is still remembered with affection by those in the North East. Although Ayresome Park is long gone (replaced by a housing estate called 'The Turnstile', which I'm almost 100 per cent sure sounds more picturesque than it is), there is a small bronze cast of a footprint that sits in front of where the old Holgate End would be, marking the exact spot where Pak Doo-Ik launched his unforgettable goal-bound strike. Needless to say, it doesn't get many Italian visitors (or North Koreans, for that matter ...).

Tofik Bakhramov, 1966

Ask anyone but a diehard football fan what Tofik Bakhramov's contribution to World Cup history was and you'll be sure to be greeted with a quizzical look. But follow it up with the words 'the Russian linesman' and suddenly the light bulb will go on and the tale of the 'Was it?/Wasn't it?' goal of 1966 will burst into life.

Azerbaijan-born Bakhramov made the most famous and controversial decision in World Cup history when, during extra time in the 1966 World Cup Final between England and West Germany, he adjudged Geoff Hurst's shot on goal to have bounced behind the goal-line after hitting the crossbar in the 100th minute. Not only did the decision give England a crucial 3–2 lead and propel them to their first, and only, World Cup win, but it sparked thousands of conspiracy theories, pub arguments and TV shows about whether the ball actually crossed the line. There's never been definitive video or photographic evidence of which side the ball bounced on — just the word of one of the few men who were looking in the right direction as events took place.

Bakhramov enjoyed no small measure of fame for his decision. Said to have been awarded a golden whistle by the queen 'for services to England', he was feted at home for bringing global attention to Azerbaijan (they even produced a stamp with his face on it), and the national stadium in Baku was renamed the Tofik Bakhramov Stadium in his honour. In 2004, ahead of a World Cup qualifier between England and Azerbaijan, a statue of the official was unveiled, while visiting England fans laid flowers on his grave in tribute. England's hat-trick hero, Hurst, was in attendance for the ceremony and said: 'On behalf of the whole of England, I would like to thank the family of Tofik Bakhramov.'

RIP Tofik Bakhramov — a true English hero.

Jairzinho, Brazil 1966, 1970, 1974

Although he played for more than two decades and appeared in three World Cup finals, Brazil maestro Jairzinho will always be remembered for what he achieved in 1970. Playing predominantly on the right wing, but often drifting inside to take up positions more akin to an out-and-out centre forward, Jairzinho became the first player to score in every game of a World Cup finals, earning him the nickname 'The Hurricane of Mexico 70'.

After a brace against Czechoslovakia in the opening match, he netted against England, Romania, Peru and Uruguay before scoring his country's third in the 4–1 win over Italy in the final. His seven goals are a pretty special collection, full of pace, trickery and a rocket of a right foot. That he scored them all while playing as a right-winger speaks much to his adaptability, as he was actually a No.10 by trade: 'I was a deep-lying attacker, a No.10,' he told FIFA.com.

> **Together in that side we had five players who practically carried out the same role for their clubs. We were all No.10s. Your position was more or less determined by your shirt number. I wore No.7, which was right-wing. Rivelino, with No.11, was on the left. And, as it turned out, we all attacked.**

In addition to his historic exploits under the Mexican sun, Jairzinho also holds a unique place in the lineage of Brazilian footballing greats. As a teenager he joined Botafogo and was groomed to replace the legendary Garrincha, which he did with much aplomb after 'The Little Bird' left in 1965. Then as a coach in the early '90s, he discovered a young Ronaldo Luís Nazário de Lima and was instrumental in the future World Cup legend being offered his first contract by Cruzeiro.

Mwepu Ilunga, Zaire 1974

Mwepu Ilunga's infamous World Cup moment has been replayed thousands of times, usually as a punchline on a 'World Cup's Craziest Moments' TV special. As Brazil waited to take a free kick in their 1974 group game against Zaire, Ilunga suddenly ran out from the wall and thumped the ball upfield, to the amazement of everyone in the Parkstadion in Gelsenkirchen. The crowd, and even a couple of the Brazil players, cracked up laughing as the referee showed the defender a yellow card. The kick was later ridiculed as an example of African football's naiveté on the world stage. However, the events leading up to the wild hack that brought so much comic relief over the years has far more sinister undertones; the reality was that Ilunga and his Zairean teammates were in fear of their lives.

Playing under the watchful eye of cold-blooded dictator President Mobutu, initial promises of financial rewards for the players were replaced with threats against their lives and families, especially ahead of the final group game against Brazil, which came off the back of a 9–0 thrashing to Yugoslavia. Angry at the shame the players had brought upon his nation, Mobutu had told the team that if they lost by 4–0 or worse, they wouldn't see their families again; against that background, and with Ilunga's wild hack coming at 2–0 down against a clearly superior opponent, the moment suddenly doesn't seem so funny. Many observers called Ilunga's actions a publicity stunt or a craving for five minutes of fame but, as he told writer John Spurling in *Death or Glory: The Dark History of the World Cup*, 'stupid pranks weren't uppermost in my mind'. At the very least, his punt wasted a few valuable seconds and gave him and his teammates a lifeline.

Ilunga's true reasons for the boneheaded kick remained a mystery for nearly forty years, and when he finally spoke about it, in a BBC radio interview in 2010, it was slightly disappointing to hear that money — namely the unpaid bonuses and wages promised by Mobutu — was the motivating factor.

> **I was aware of football regulations but I did [the kick] deliberately. I did not have a reason to continue playing and getting injured while those who would benefit financially were sitting on the terraces watching. Why should I continue playing while other people are getting paid for it? I prefer to do that and get a red card than continue playing. I knew the rules very well but the referee was quite lenient and only gave me a yellow card. I don't regret it at all.**

Mario Kempes, Argentina 1974, 1978, 1982

It seems a little strange that a player who was never booked or sent off in his career would have the nickname '*El Matador*', or 'The Killer', but Mario Kempes's sobriquet was all about his ability to put the ball in the back of the net, something he did more times than anyone else in the 1978 World Cup finals, as Argentina became world champions for the first time.

A disappointing outing in the 1974 finals gave no indication that Kempes would become a dominant tournament player, and opinions weren't changed when he drew a blank in the group stages in 1978. He certainly had the pedigree; as the only European-based player in César Luis Menotti's squad, the twenty-four-year-old was a two-time La Liga top scorer with Valencia.

It eventually took a change of venue to the friendly confines of Rosario — where he scored eighty-five goals in 107 games for Rosario Central between 1974 and 1976 — to really kickstart Kempes's tournament. He scored both goals against Poland and grabbed another brace in the controversial game against Peru to send Argentina to the final against the Netherlands, where his double saw off the *Oranje* 3–1 in extra time. His first goal was a fantastic poacher's finish, slipping the ball under the onrushing Jan Jongbloed, while his second was a scrappy toe-poke after his initial shot bounced up off the keeper.

Winner of the Golden Boot and Player of the Tournament in 1978, not even a poor showing in the 1982 finals could dull the memory of one of Argentina's all-time greats, a man that Diego Maradona said 'put Argentinean football on the map'. Kempes himself was more modest of his place in the pantheon of his nation's greats: 'My country is extremely fortunate in that it produces great footballers. I am just one of many who have played their part in Argentina's football history'.

Paolo Rossi, Italy 1978, 1982 and Salvatore Schillaci, Italy 1990

The World Cup has been very kind to Italian strikers, especially those who weren't supposed to play for Italy in the World Cup. Take Paolo Rossi and Salvatore 'Totò' Schillaci, for example, two players who by all rights should never have taken the field for the *Azzurri* but who inspired their nation to great heights when they did.

The call-up of striker Paolo Rossi to the Italian side by Enzo Bearzot raised more than a few eyebrows in 1982, as the Juve man had played just three games after returning from a two-year match-fixing ban. It looked like Bearzot had made a blunder when Italy barely scraped through their qualifying group (scoring only two goals) to face the might of Brazil and Argentina in the next stage, but the coach kept his faith and Rossi repaid it in spades with a stunning hat-trick against Brazil. The 3–2 win was an all-time classic and would have cemented Rossi's place in World Cup history on its own, but the twenty-five-year-old wasn't finished. In the semifinal against Poland, Rossi grabbed two more and then opened the scoring in the final against West Germany in their 3–1 win at the Bernabéu. The diminutive striker was the toast of Italy, becoming the first player to take home the Golden Boot, Golden Ball and a winners' medal in the same tournament.

Eight years later, on home soil at Italia 90, another *Azzurri* striker emerged from nowhere to become the saviour of Italian football. Salvatore 'Totò' Schillaci was even more of a long shot to make the Italian side than Rossi, playing Serie B football a year before and only making his debut for the national side three months before the tournament kicked off. In a real-life fairytale, 'Totò' scored four minutes after coming on as a sub against Austria — his first competitive match for Italy — and then scored a crucial winner against Ireland in the knockout stages. He also found the net in the semifinal against Argentina, which Italy would go on to lose on penalties, and in the third-place playoff against England to win the Golden Boot.

'I was asked by Roberto Baggio to take the penalty — he said, "You take it and you can be top scorer",' said Schillaci. 'I accepted the offer from Baggio and with the penalty I won the Golden Boot.'

In total Schillaci's international career lasted only eighteen months, but for those magical summer nights in 1990 where he was the darling of world football, it is one most players would take in a heartbeat.

Zico, Brazil 1978, 1982, 1986

Brazil's 1982 team is seen by many as the greatest team never to win the World Cup — and that Zico was viewed as that team's best player says all you need to know about his place as one of his country's all-time greats. The Flamengo midfielder was the *Seleçao*'s creative focal point in the 1980s, dictating the pace and rhythm of the game, carving up defences with pinpoint passes and chipping in with the odd spectacular goal, too.

Arthur Antunes Coimbra, to give Zico his birth name, first played in the World Cup in 1978 and, despite some unspectacular performances by a team lacking the typical Brazilian flair, it proved to be his best-ever finish in the tournament (third). The twenty-five-year-old struggled to make his mark in the side and was best known for his headed 'goal' from a corner in the final seconds against Sweden, which was disallowed by referee Clive Thomas when he whistled for full-time while the ball was in mid-air.

By the 1982 finals, Zico had established himself as one of the stars of Brazilian football, earning himself the often-used nickname 'The White Pelé', and coach Tele Santana's side were favourites to win the title. Featuring the attacking talent of Falcão, Socrates and Junior, they swept aside their group stage opponents with a festival of flair, punctuated by Zico's stunning bicycle kick against New Zealand and sublime free kick against Scotland.

In the second group stage, Brazil made short work of rivals Argentina and needed only a draw against Italy to progress to the semis. In the first half, Zico was at his best, pulling the strings in the midfield and setting up Socrates' first goal with a brilliant turn and pass. But as the game wore on, and as Italy's Claudio Gentile kicked at any available appendage, Zico's influence waned and Paolo Rossi's hat-trick saw the *Azzurri* through 3–2. One of Brazil's all-time great teams was out of the tournament, and many blamed Zico for not being able to assert more control on proceedings.

The 1986 finals proved no happier hunting ground for Brazil or Zico. After topping their group and beating Poland 4–0 in the second round, Brazil went out to a talented French side on penalties in the quarterfinal. Zico missed a penalty in regulation time that could have proved the difference, and despite holding his nerve in the shootout, teammates Socrates and Júlio César couldn't, and France triumphed 4–3.

Although he continued to play for Flamengo until 1990, Mexico was Zico's last World Cup as a player. A move to Japan saw him become instrumental in the growth of the domestic game as a player and coach at Kashima Antlers and, after a brief return to Brazil, he took the job as coach of the Japan national team in 2002, guiding them to the 2006 finals in Germany.

The 1982 World Cup plays heavily on the minds of Brazil's players and fans who watched such an exciting team fail to meet expectations, and it's clear that after many years, the defeat to Italy still has its scars: 'It's always important to leave a legacy, but what matters to a professional is the title,' said Zico. 'I'm happy to have been part of a team like that, though, and people everywhere still remember us. But I'd be even happier if we'd have won.'

Michel Platini, France 1978, 1982, 1986

In the early 1980s, Frenchman Michel Platini was the best player in the world. His tactical awareness, superb technique and remarkable range of passing were allied to an uncanny ability to find the net from an advanced midfield position; in short, he was the complete attacking package.

A winner of French and Italian titles and several European honours with Juventus, that Platini never won the World Cup is one of the great injustices in the game (up there with Cruyff's lack of World Cup coronation). Unfortunately for '*Platoche*', both he and his national team peaked in the years between two World Cup finals; Platini was named European Footballer of the Year in 1983, 1984 and 1985 and, inspired by their talismanic captain's nine goals in five matches, France won the 1984 European Championships.

Not that Platini needed a winner's medal to be considered a World Cup great. He made his debut in the 1978 tournament, although he had little chance to make an impact in a 'Group of Death' that featured eventual champions Argentina and Italy. However, in 1982, France had a team to be reckoned with, as midfielders Platini, Luis Fernández, Jean Tigana and Alain Giresse formed the *carré magique*, or 'magic square', to devastating effect.

Leaving his goalscoring boots at home (he scored only twice), Platini was still at the centre of all things France created, constantly probing and guiding. However, a place in the history books was snatched away by West Germany in a highly exciting — and controversial — semifinal won on a penalty shootout. Platini scored the equalising penalty and was also at the side of fallen teammate Patrick Battiston as he was stretchered off the field after a clash with the West Germany keeper. 'That night I went through a scaled-down version of a lifetime's worth of emotion,' he would later reveal.

As reigning European champions, expectations were high for France in 1986 — but Platini endured a subdued tournament as *Les Bleus* fell in the semifinal to West Germany for the second consecutive tournament. The thirty-year-old showed flashes of his brilliant best, especially against Italy in a 2–0 second round win, but West Germany proved fitter and more organised in their 2–1 semifinal win.

After retiring from the game in 1987, Platini took over the French national side for five years before moving into the administrative side of the game, first as the co-president of the French Organising Committee for the 1998 World Cup and then as the President of UEFA, a position he has held since 2007.

Roger Milla, Cameroon 1982, 1990, 1994

At thirty-eight years old, most footballers have disappeared into a retirement of golf, shopping and bad punditry. For Cameroon's Roger Milla, he hadn't even enjoyed his finest footballing moments yet.

A highly decorated player in his home country — he won the CAF Cup Winners' Cup and the African Player of the Year Award, and led Cameroon to their first-ever World Cup appearance in

1982 — Milla initially struggled to establish himself in French football, bouncing from club to club in the late '80s. After successful stints at Saint-Étienne and Montpellier (sixty-eight goals in 154 appearances for the two clubs), Milla hung up his boots in 1989 and retired to Reunion Island in the Indian Ocean.

And that should've been the last we heard of Milla — except for the fact Cameroon qualified for Italia 90 and, with the side in disarray, a personal call from President Paul Biya convinced the thirty-eight-year-old to come out of retirement for one last swan song.

And what a swan song it was, the old man coming off the bench in five games to light up the tournament with swashbuckling goals and a hip-shimmying *makossa* celebration that would quickly achieve cult status. He netted twice against Romania (becoming the World Cup's oldest goalscorer in the process) and scored two more against Colombia in extra time to set up a quarterfinal against England. In a tense affair, he almost turned the game for the Indomitable Lions, winning a penalty and setting up Eugène Ekeke to give Cameroon the lead, only for two late penalties from Gary Lineker to reverse the result.

Amazingly, forty-two-year-old Milla was back again in 1994, breaking his own oldest-player scoring record with a strike against Russia and becoming the first African to play in three World Cup tournaments.

When asked by *France Football* for his enduring image of the 1990 World Cup, Milla overlooked personal achievements to note the image of Cameroon president Biya shaking hands with other world leaders after the opening game victory over Argentina.

> **Can you appreciate that? An African head of state who leaves as the victor, and who greets with a smile the defeated heads of state ... It's thanks to football that a small country could become great.**

Lothar Matthäus, West Germany/Germany 1982, 1986, 1990, 1994, 1998

With a record twenty-five appearances spread out over five tournaments, few national teams' performances at the World Cup have been so intertwined with that of a player as Germany's was with Lothar Matthäus. A polarising figure for his arrogance and outspokenness, there was no denying that on the pitch 'Der Terminator' was one of the best players of his generation.

Called up into the German squad for the 1982 finals, Matthäus played understudy to the great Paul Breitner in Spain and only managed a couple of substitute appearances as West Germany lost the final to Italy. A move from Borussia Mönchengladbach to Bayern Munich in 1984 saw Matthäus establish himself as one of the best attacking midfielders in world football, winning Bundesliga titles in his first two seasons at the club. In the 1986 finals the twenty-five-year-old was one of the first names on Franz Beckenbauer's team sheet, and his partnership with Felix Magath in the middle of the park propelled West Germany to the final against Argentina. Given the assignment of marking Diego Maradona — a task that did not play to his strengths — Matthäus worked diligently to keep the Argentinean in check, but it was not enough to stop him from setting up the winning goal in the *albiceleste*'s 3–2 win in the Azteca Stadium.

Italia 90 witnessed Matthäus at the peak of his game. His dynamic, inspirational performances for *die Mannschaft* saw him hit the net four times en route to another final showdown against Argentina, the standout being his second long-range pile-driver against Yugoslavia, one of the goals of the tournament. Rated by Maradona as his biggest rival, West Germany's captain was not going to let the South American genius get the better of him twice and, in a poor final, Matthäus finally got the winner's medal he'd come so close to winning on two previous occasions.

1990 was the high-water mark for both player and country and, as Matthäus's powers declined, so did German football.

A knee injury forced a shift to sweeper for the 1994 finals in the USA, but an ageing side were found out in the quarterfinal by an inspired Bulgaria. By then, a series of injuries had blighted the end of his career — but the thirty-seven-year-old earned one more call-up in 1998, making four more appearances including the 3–0 defeat to Croatia that finally brought the curtain down on his World Cup career.

Matthäus has spent retirement coaching in places as far flung as Serbia, Israel and South America, and was in the news in October 2013 when a court letter was stamped 'deceased' when authorities failed to contact him. The country panicked, but it proved to be a false alarm.

'This is outrageous. Everyone can see I'm alive, whether on TV or on the pitch,' said the fifty-two-year-old, who is presumably also alive when not on TV or the pitch too.

Paul Gascoigne, England 1990

For most England fans, the enduring image of the 1990 World Cup was Paul 'Gazza' Gascoigne's waterworks at the final whistle of their semifinal loss to West Germany. It was an emotional end to a finals that Gascoigne made an indelible mark on, guiding England to its best World Cup finish since 1966 and setting himself on a career path that would see him return to Italy with a big-money move to Lazio.

Only earning a place in the English squad after a Man of the Match performance in an April friendly against Czechoslovakia, Gascoigne's audacity and intelligence fashioned winners against Egypt and Belgium in the finals, giving the Three Lions a creativity not seen for a generation. There was a youthful exuberance about Gazza, the cheeky English-bloke equivalent of Maradona's *pibe*, that made him hard not to like. Despite even his coach Bobby Robson calling him 'daft as a fucking brush', his strong, assured performances were the driving force behind England making it to the semifinal and a showdown with the old enemy, West Germany. Ahead of the game, German coach Franz Beckenbauer expressed his concern about Gazza's influence on the game, stating he was 'smart, defiant and bold, like the leader of a children's gang. Behind his angular forehead, he could cook up ideas you didn't expect'.

Gascoigne was a man on a mission in the semifinal, nut-megging West Germany captain Lothar Matthäus at one point and reaching deep into his bag of tricks to try and drag England to the final. At 1–1 after ninety minutes, Gazza's defining moment came in extra time when he rashly dived in on Thomas Berthold and suddenly realised his yellow card would mean he would miss the final.

'Once I knew I was going to miss the final, you could see how heartbroken I was,' Gascoigne told the BBC. 'I just couldn't stop the tears.' Although he pulled himself together enough to make it to the penalty shootout, the waterworks couldn't be stopped for long and pictures of Gazza, tears in his eyes, pulling up the hem of his shirt and kissing it became one of the lasting images of the 1990 finals.

Although they didn't realise it at the time, Gascoigne and his teammates paved the way for English top-flight football to become a global money-making behemoth that night, the renewed popularity of the game in England contributing to the formation of the Premier League in 1992 and the lifting of the European ban on English clubs after the Heysel Stadium disaster.

Gascoigne's dream of making a second World Cup final in 1998 ended when then–England boss Glen Hoddle informed him in the team's Spanish hotel that he had not made the squad, leading to the midfielder wrecking the room while the coach watched in disbelief. Unfortunately, in retirement Gascoigne has struggled with alcoholism and allegations of domestic abuse, and has had several stints in rehab in recent years.

Oleg Salenko, Russia 1994

In the seminal basketball buddy movie *White Men Can't Jump*, Wesley Snipes's character turns to Woody Harrelson's after he loses to him one-on-one and says: 'Even the sun shines on a dog's ass some days.' It seems an appropriate adage to describe Russia's Oleg Salenko, who emerged from obscurity with a record-breaking performance and then slunk back into anonymity virtually as soon as the final whistle was blown.

Salenko's moment in the sun took place on 28 June 1994 at Stanford Stadium in San Francisco when he became the first player to score five goals in a game during a meaningless final group match against Cameroon. (Both teams had already been eliminated.) His five-goal haul broke a fifty-six-year-old tournament record and gave him a share of the Golden Boot (with Bulgaria's Hristo Stoichkov), making him the first player to be knocked out in the group stage and still win the award. Salenko didn't score a single goal outside the 1994 finals and the Cameroon game proved to be the last of his nine appearances for the national team, which the striker blamed on Russia's new coach:

> "The team's new manager, Oleg Romantsev, didn't like the fact that I had a bigger reputation than him. He preferred players that he knew, so he gradually started to drop me."

Obscurity is a relative concept, of course, as Salenko went on to play club football for another seven years in Spain, Scotland and Turkey, but as far as international football goes, the sun only shone on Salenko's hind quarters for one brief but wonderful day.

Yordan Letchkov, Bulgaria 1994

Although Hristo Stoichkov was the catalyst for Bulgaria's fairytale march to the semifinals in 1994, it was midfielder Yordan Letchkov who was the Lions' cult hero. Instantly recognisable for his bald head with the tiny soul patch at the front, it was Letchkov's 78th-minute header that capped a stunning come-from-behind win against Germany in New Jersey. But 'The Magician' was more than just a gravity-defying baldy in USA 94; his assured performances in midfield helped inspire a team who had never won a World Cup game to beat heavyweights Argentina in the group stages and see off holders Germany in the most dramatic of fashions.

Bulgaria were a disparate bunch, packed full of mavericks who were just as happy to fight each other in the dressing room as they were to share a beer and a fag the day before a game. Which is exactly what they did before the big clash with Germany, celebrating Letchkov's birthday with a few cold ones and some sunbathing by the hotel pool.

'We combined work and pleasure,' Letchkov told *FourFourTwo*.

> **❝I remember that the FBI were providing our security services and every day for forty-five days, they would see us have a drink, smoke a cigarette or go to a bar. When we left they said they would miss us and they weren't joking.❞**

Having scored the decisive penalty shootout spot-kick in the Round of 16 game against Mexico, Letchkov was at the centre of the action in the showdown with Germany, giving away a 47th-minute penalty by breathing on dive-happy centre forward Jürgen Klinsmann. But after Stoichkov's beautiful free kick put The Lions back on level terms with fifteen minutes to go, Letchkov made amends by launching himself at a Zlatko Yankov cross and bulleting a header past Bodo Illgner.

It was the high point of the World Cup for Bulgaria, who lost 2–1 to Italy in the semifinal and were then whipped 4–0 by Sweden in the third/fourth match, but Letchkov prefers to remember the hero's welcome the team received when they returned home.

'The way we were greeted on our return to Sofia was unbelievable. A player can only dream about receiving such love and passion from people.'

As for Letchkov's famous hairstyle, his renown was such that Tibetan monks were said to be sporting 'Letchkovs' — but in reality he only possessed the third-best coiffure in the team. Number one had to be wig-wearing goalkeeper Borislav Mikhailov, who could be seen adjusting his hairpiece after it slipped off his sweaty dome in the game against Mexico, closely followed by Trifon Ivanov, whose mullet and bulgy eyes made him look like the lovechild of Marty Feldman and Lurch from *The Addams Family*. Google him at your peril.

Lilian Thuram, France 1998, 2002, 2006

If you're only ever going to score two goals in your international career, you might as well make them big ones. Lilian Thuram's two strikes against Croatia in the 1998 semifinal turned a 1–0 deficit into a 2–1 victory, and gave *Les Bleus* a place in the final against Brazil. Although Zinedine Zidane garnered all the headlines at the conclusion of France 98, the Guadeloupe-born fullback was arguably France's best player, providing much-needed width and attacking impetus to a team that struggled to consistently find the net.

His *pièce de résistance* came in the semifinal against surprise-package Croatia, who had knocked out Germany in the previous round. Croatia were powered by the goals of Davor Suker, and when the Real Madrid man put them ahead with a clinical strike in the 46th minute, the chances of France overturning the deficit with their misfiring strikers looked bleak. But no-one had accounted for the attacking prowess of Thuram. (And why would they, seeing as he hadn't scored for France before ... and never would again?)

Thuram's first goal came just a minute after Croatia's opener (where he was the defender responsible for playing goalscorer Suker onside), as he dispossessed Zvonimir Boban on the edge of the Croatia box and exchanged passes with Youri Djorkaeff to calmly side-foot home. Twenty minutes later Thuram was at it again, out-muscling Robert Jarni and then hitting a sweet left-foot drive into the bottom corner of Drazen Ladic's goal. His pensive 'man in thought' celebration struck a great contrast to the madness taking place around him, and he was soon engulfed by euphoric teammates who realised they'd just witnessed history.

Thuram went on to win the World Cup four days later, and the 2000 European Championships, but nothing would match the events of that night at the Stade de France — not that he can remember any of it. Coach Aimé Jacquet said Thuram was in a 'mystical state', and the defender himself has very little recollection of events.

'It was like a trance,' he admitted in an interview with *The Guardian*.

> **I still have no recollection of what happened and, even though I try, I still can't put it together. I needed Aimé Jacquet and the other players to tell me that we had won, and that we were in the World Cup Final.**

Andrés Iniesta, Spain 2010

Spain's 2010 run to the final, where they overcame the negative tactics and barely disguised thuggery of the Netherlands to win the trophy, was as close to a complete team performance as has been seen in the World Cup.

Although criticised in some circles for not being adventurous or creating enough chances — they reached the final having scored the fewest number of goals in history (seven) — Spain's tactics were always more about controlling the game with possession than producing goalscoring opportunities. With the majority of their players hailing from two clubs — Barcelona and Real Madrid — *La Roja* enjoyed the advantage of familiarity, but at the very heart of their performances there still needed to be a playmaker of supreme skill to orchestrate proceedings. That man was Andrés Iniesta.

Snapped up by the Barcelona youth academy as a pale and skinny twelve-year-old, Iniesta dazzled coaches with his natural ability, prompting coach Pep Guardiola to say he had found a player 'who reads the game better than me'. The young boy had it all — vision, speed, skill and a strength that belied his 5 foot 7 frame — and it took only four years at La Masia before he began training with the Barça first team.

Making his first-team debut in 2002, Iniesta made an immediate connection with teammate Xavi and, although he struggled to nail down a first-team place under coach Frank Rijkaard, he became the creative focal point of arguably the best club team in football history under Pep Guardiola. Barcelona won fourteen trophies in four seasons, including three successive La Liga titles and two Champions League trophies.

For Spain, Iniesta has been equally influential, guiding the national team to consecutive European Championships titles in 2008 and 2012, winning the Player of the Tournament Award in the latter. But the high point came in the 2010 World Cup finals, where he followed up on several masterful performances by scoring the winning goal in the final against the Netherlands.

Growing in stature as the game progressed, Iniesta began to take control of the final in the second half and extra time, but it took a Netherlands red card to change the outcome of the game. Johnny Heitinga's dismissal led to a defensive reshuffle for the Netherlands, and the subbing off of Nigel de Jong finally gave Iniesta the time and space he needed to make a breakthrough. With four minutes to go, a quick through-ball from Cesc Fàbregas found Iniesta bearing down on the right side of the goal and, after one touch to bring the ball under control, he buried the volley past keeper Maarten Stekelenburg's outstretched glove.

It says much about Iniesta the man that, even while celebrating the greatest moment of his career, he still had the presence of mind to pay tribute to former international teammate Dani Jarque, who had died of a heart attack a year before; his t-shirt was inscribed with the words 'Dani Jarque. *Siempre con nosotros.'* — 'Dani Jarque. Always with us.' It spoke to Iniesta's more sensitive side, the one that saw him 'cry rivers' when his parents left him at La Masia and prompted him to note his sadness at natural disasters such as the Australian floods and the Japanese earthquakes.

But don't get it twisted — he might be the man with a heart of gold and unassuming manner, but when he crosses the white line he's a stone-cold killer in studs. Just ask any Dutchman.

6

THE WORLD CUP'S GREATEST GAMES

Pitting the planet's best teams against each other in a tournament to find the world champion is not always a guarantee of great football. The pressure exerted by the World Cup — the weight of expectation from fans and media, the physical and mental toll top-class football takes on an athlete, and living in virtual lock-down for weeks on end — can lead to some pretty average games. Being bored to tears by at least one World Cup game is as inevitable as a cameraman panning to a woman in a bikini top at a Brazil game or FIFA president Sepp Blatter making some stupid comment about women or race.

But the threat of partial brain paralysis is not enough to stop most fans from tuning in to each and every game. Any veteran World Cup fan will attest that, just when you're least expecting it, the tournament will throw a rip-roaring classic at you. Usually there's no rhyme or reason for when a great game will land in your lap. It's just as likely to be two already-knocked-out minnows playing for pride as it is two heavyweights fighting for a place in the finals. The great part is you never know when the next one will be, and that's why we remain glued to our TV sets for three weeks.

Over its nineteen-tournament history, the World Cup has had its fair share of cracking games — from the first final in Montevideo to the highly charged clash between old enemies England and Argentina in 1998 — and has featured such oddities as players concussed by their celebrating teammates, kamikaze German keepers, and a blubbering defender told by a teammate to stop crying in the middle of the game or risk getting a thump in the face.

Uruguay 4 Argentina 2
World Cup Final, 30 July 1930, Estadio Centenario, Montevideo, Uruguay

Going into the tournament there might have been question marks over Uruguay hosting the first World Cup finals, but by the day of the first final there was no denying FIFA had got the venue right. Aided by the fact that the showcase event would be fought out by neighbouring countries separated by a short ferry ride, the atmosphere in Montevideo before kickoff was at fever pitch as fans of Uruguay and Argentina descended on the Estadio Centenario. Tens of thousands of Argentineans had made the trip over by boat — although one group of fans got lost in fog and weren't found until the next day — and tensions were high ahead of the game. More than 150,000 turned up at the stadium, which had a capacity of 90,000, and both sets of fans showed immense national pride, with scenes of singing, goading and fighting commonplace.

The players were feeling the heat as much as the fans. Both teams were escorted to the stadium by armed guards, and Argentina captain Luis Monti later revealed that he had been sent death threats. Even Belgian referee John Langenus demanded a police escort for after the game, in case things got out of control. While the crowd behaved itself on the whole, the same couldn't be said for the two teams, who argued about whose ball they were going to use (Uruguayans had slightly larger balls than Argentineans, apparently). Langenus decided the only way to resolve the issue was to have a coin toss, which Argentina won, but the home side dug their heels in and demanded the second half be played with their ball, which it was.

Led by captain José Nasazzi, double Olympic champs Uruguay were the favourites, but Argentina had a forward line — featuring stars Carlos Peucelle and Guillermo Stábile — that could unlock the tightest of defences. The first half was action packed, with Uruguay taking the lead through Pablo Dorado.

Argentina quickly fought back though, and Peucelle levelled the score after a great team move, before Stábile put the visitors into the lead ten minutes from half-time. While the goal was hotly disputed for offside, it was no more than Argentina deserved, as they dominated large portions of the game. The Centenario crowd were stunned into silence.

The second half belonged to Uruguay, who turned the game on its head with three sparkling goals (they clearly liked playing with their own balls rather than Argentina's). First Pedro Cea scored the leveller after a long dribble, then Victoriano Iriarte put them ahead with a long-range strike; Hector Castro wrapped things up with a goal in the 89th minute. The stronger team had won out, although Argentina were hampered by an injury to Pancho Varallo (with no subs allowed, he could only stand out on the wing) and an ineffective performance by Luis Monti, who was clearly shaken by the threats made on his life.

Uruguay became the first nation to win the World Cup and the party on the streets of Montevideo lasted well into the early hours (luckily the following day was declared a national holiday); in contrast, the ferry ride back for the Argentinean fans was long and painful. The World Cup had arrived.

Brazil 6 Poland 5 (a.e.t.)
First Round, 5 June 1938, Stade de la Meinau, Strasbourg, France

If the start of Brazil's love affair with the World Cup can be traced to one game, the 1938 first-round clash against Poland would be it. The match had it all: eleven goals, massive swings in momentum, a pitch like a Glastonbury field and not one but *two* hat-trick heroes.

Brazil might not have been 'Brazil' yet, but in Leônidas they had a player who captured the imagination and became the World Cup's first superstar. 'The Black Diamond' was an elastic-legged forward who could do virtually anything with the ball (he was said to have invented the bicycle kick) — and what he did with it against Poland was put it in the net a lot of times. But although his efforts saw Brazil emerge triumphant after extra time, the bandy-legged South American wasn't even the game's highest scorer — that honour went to Poland's Ernest Wilimowski. (Told you this game had everything.)

The conditions were wet and the pitch was muddy in Strasbourg, but that didn't put the two teams off laying on a goal-scoring feast. Brazil might have been cruising at 3–1 at the break thanks to goals from Leônidas, Romeu and Perácio, but no-one factored in the will and determination of blond bombshell Wilimowski, who scored a second-half hat-trick — including an 89th-minute equaliser — to send the game to extra time at 4–4.

If the second half was Wilimowski's, then extra time was owned by 'The Rubber Man'. He scored three minutes into the added stanza, despite losing a boot in the mud in the build-up, and then made sure of the result with his hat-trick strike on 104 minutes. Not even a historic fourth from Wilimowski could save Poland from losing what is still the closest double digit–goal game in World Cup history.

One interesting footnote to the match is the debate as to whether Leônidas actually equalled Wilimowski's tally of four goals in the game. Several well-researched books differ on how many and even when Leônidas scored his three or four goals: Brian Glanville's interminably dull *The Story of the World Cup* has the Brazilian scoring a hat-trick in the first half alone, while FIFA's official website has him scoring one in the first half and two in extra time, with no mention of a fourth. Who to trust: a journalist or FIFA?

Hungary 4 Uruguay 2 (a.e.t.)

Semifinal, 30 June 1954, La Pontaise Stadium, Lausanne, Switzerland

Hungary's following game — the 'Miracle of Bern' final against West Germany — may be more famous, but the Magical Magyars' semifinal clash against Uruguay was by far the better game. Hungary were undefeated for nearly four years, and defending champions Uruguay had never lost a World Cup game going into this match; it was the classic example of an unstoppable force against an immovable object.

There was little to separate the two teams; Hungary were the best team in the world, despite their reputation having taken a knock due to their 'Battle of Bern' game against Brazil, and Uruguay were buoyed by a 4–2 quarterfinal victory over England after topping their group. The only sour point was that both teams were without their best player — Hungary's Ferenc Puskás and Uruguay's Obdulio Varela were out injured.

So it was more than a little surprising that Hungary jumped out to a 2–0 lead early in the second half thanks to two goals from the irrepressible Nándor Hidegkuti. Uruguay were the more energetic of the two teams, but Hungary's slick interplay, especially in the final third, was proving the difference. *La Celeste* would not lay down, though, and a manic final fifteen minutes saw Juan Alberto Schiaffino and Juan Hohberg run riot, with the latter scoring twice in quick succession to level the tie. (He was said to have been knocked out by his over-excited teammates while celebrating the 87th-minute equaliser.)

Hohberg could have been the hero of the hour had his shot not hit the woodwork in the first period of extra time, but it was the closest his team came to scoring. While a Uruguay defender was receiving treatment behind the goal, Sándor Kocsis headed Hungary into the lead and he sealed the deal with another header seven minutes from time. After the game, both teams recognised the epic battle they had been in, and, while it would be scant consolation to Uruguay, Hungary manager Gyula Mándi admitted: 'We beat the best team we have ever met.'

Portugal 5 North Korea 3
Quarterfinal, 23 July 1966, Goodison Park, Liverpool, England

On paper, the quarterfinal clash between Portugal and North Korea seemed a mismatch of epic proportions. The Portugese side were made up of several of the legendary Benfica side of the mid-'60s, and in Eusébio they could boast the most exciting and dynamic player in the tournament. North Korea, on the other hand, were in uncharted territory; having shocked Italy 1–0 in the previous round, they were suddenly the English crowd's second-favourite team — but they weren't tipped to put up much resistance against a strong European side.

Not that North Korea had much time to resist in the opening minutes, as they were too busy scoring up the other end; attacking at every opportunity, they found themselves 3–0 up within twenty-five minutes. Pak Seung-Zin's first-minute effort crashed off the underside of the crossbar and in, and it was followed by Li Dong-Woon's half-volley on the counterattack twenty minutes later. Yang Seung-Kook fashioned a third goal, and all of a sudden North Korea's dream of making a World Cup semifinal looked to be coming true.

Unfortunately, North Korea's dreams were about to become a nightmare courtesy of Eusébio, who seemed almost personally affronted by the temerity of his opponents. Taking the game over almost singlehandedly, he clawed two goals back before half-time, each time running to pick the ball out of the goal and place it back in the centre circle. 'The Black Pearl' continued his tear in the second half with two more goals, his fourth a penalty after a scintillating run down the left wing was ended with a hack in the box. To round things off, he even turned provider for the final Portugal goal, hitting in a corner that led to José Augusto's header that ended any hope of a Korea comeback.

The ease with which Eusébio tore North Korea's defence apart that day at Goodison Park made for compelling viewing, and his performance lives on as one of the greatest-ever individual

World Cup efforts. That the North Korean side left English shores with nearly as much acclaim said much about their accomplishments too.

Italy 4 West Germany 3 (a.e.t.)
Semifinal, 17 June 1970, Estadio Azteca, Mexico City, Mexico

The 1970 semifinal between Italy and Germany divides opinion among football fans. For many it lives up to its 'Game of the Century' title, with its breathtaking finale that saw six goals in twenty-one extra-time minutes; for others, the very fact that there were six goals — many of which were the result of shoddy defending — in twenty-one minutes means that it is unworthy of classic status. What the naysayers fail to see is the sheer drama of the occasion, as two teams fought tooth and nail through fatigue, injury, exhaustion and extreme heat for a place in the World Cup Final.

The Italians took the lead in the eighth minute, thanks to a snap shot from Roberto Boninsegna squeezing its way inside Sepp Maier's right-hand post. Thinking one was enough, the *Azzurri* decided to shut up shop — but that was easier said than done against a frontline of Uwe Seeler and Gerd Müller. Germany came forward in waves, but either the brilliant keeping of Enrico Albertosi, the woodwork (Wolfgang Overath hit the crossbar) or the referee (a 67th-minute foul on Franz Beckenbauer was controversially deemed to be outside the box) denied them a goal. That was, until Karl-Heinz Schnellinger poked home a Jürgen Grabowski cross in added time; for the first time in the game Italy's defenders were nowhere, and Germany made them pay.

A tight and defensive first ninety minutes gave no indication of the flood of goals that were coming in the last thirty, although the oppressive heat inside the Azteca certainly played its part in knackering the players. Germany got the goalfest started with a Müller goal that took advantage of a mix-up between Italy's defenders, but four minutes later Italy were on level terms again when Tarcisio Burgnich slammed home after some equally poor defending from Sigfried Held. Just before the end of the first period, Gigi Riva put the *Azzurri* in front with a brilliant control and finish that would have been a worthy winner to any game.

But neither team was willing to call it quits, with the constant attacks in the final fifteen minutes resembling a basketball game more than a World Cup semi. Germany equalised again through a Müller header but, before the crappy '70s graphics even had time to leave the TV screen, Italy had kicked off and scored, Gianni Rivera hitting home from a Boninsegna cross. It was to be the last goal of an electric game, as both teams were dead on their feet in the last ten minutes (especially Beckenbauer, who had the added discomfort of playing with a dislocated shoulder in extra time).

Italy emerged victorious in one of the greatest games ever played, and it came as no surprise that they had little left in the tank for the final, four days later. They went down 4–1 to Brazil.

Italy 3 Brazil 2
Second Round, 5 July 1982, Estadio Sarriá, Barcelona, Spain

The second-round group game between Italy and Brazil in Barcelona epitomised all that was good about early-1980s football: muffled commentary, really short shorts, sweat-stained cotton shirts, iconic haircuts and the adidas Tango ball. Oh, and the football on display wasn't too bad either. Actually, it was bloody brilliant.

The two teams featured players who would go down in history as their countries' very best: Brazil's Zico, Falcão and Socrates and Italy's Zoff, Gentile and Rossi. Brazil had returned to their *jogo bonito* roots after a couple of uninspiring outings, playing with a skill and flair not seen since the early '70s. They scored thirteen goals in their first four games and had an embarrassment of riches in every attacking position (although defence was another matter entirely). Italy were on the opposite end of the scale, scraping through their qualifying group on goal difference and being heavily criticised by the media back home.

Both teams saw off Argentina in what was the original 'Group of Death'. When they faced each other on a steaming hot day in Barcelona for a place in the semifinals, Telê Santana's Brazil needed a draw while Italy needed to win.

The game burst into life after just five minutes when Bruno Conti's run and pass released Antonio Cabrini to cross into Brazil's area, where Paolo Rossi ghosted in to head home virtually unchallenged. Slapped into life, Brazil's midfield took over; a breathtaking swivel and pass by Zico took out the entire Italy defence, leaving Socrates time to hit the ball low and hard past Dino Zoff. Brazil were starting to find their feet until defender Cerezo's lazy cross-field pass landed right at Paolo Rossi's, who took two touches and then blasted the ball home for his second goal of the game. (Fellow defender Junior looked across at Cerezo after the goal to see him welling up and said: 'If you don't stop crying, I'm going to smack you in the face.')

Both teams had scoring opportunities early in the second half, most notably Rossi with just the keeper to beat for a hat-trick. In the 68th minute, Brazil drew level when Falcão, cleverly using a dummy run by Cerezo, cut infield and drilled a shot past Zoff's right hand. The *Seleçao* were not a team to sit on a lead, and pushing forward for a winner proved their undoing. With fifteen minutes remaining Italy hit them on a counter and won a corner. Despite having every member of the team in the box defending, Brazil could only clear as far as Marco Tardelli, whose shot was redirected by Rossi into the net for his *tripletta*. Rossi became the toast of Italy, scoring half of his Golden Boot–winning tally of six goals and setting the *Azzurri* on a path to their third World Cup win.

The Brazilians still call the game the 'Disaster of Sarriá', while the rest of us simply remember it as a cracking game of football.

West Germany 3 France 3 (a.e.t.),
West Germany won 5–4 on penalties
Semifinal, 8 July 1982, Ramón Sánchez Pizjuán Stadium, Seville, Spain

The finals in Spain produced another first-class match but, in contrast to the 'beautiful game' between Brazil and Italy, France and West Germany was a classic good-against-evil clash.

The analogy works when comparing the teams' playing styles — France were swashbucklingly good thanks to their midfield musketeers Platini, Giresse and Tigana, while West Germany were grinders who only progressed out of their group because of a dodgy game against Austria — but it was given more meaning after the Schumacher/Battiston incident in the second half (see Chapter 8 for more) that saw the Frenchman put in a coma and the German showing little contrition for his actions.

Despite featuring some good football, the match showed few signs of being a classic in the first half. Germany took the lead through Pierre Littbarski, who followed up on Klaus Fischer's shot to blast the rebound past keeper Jean-Luc Ettori, with France levelling with a Platini penalty ten minutes later.

Then came German keeper Harald Schumacher's assault on Patrick Battiston, which deeply affected France, but not in the way many expected.

'We were psychologically affected, but in a positive sense,' Michel Platini told *FourFourTwo*. 'We were full of rage: against the Germans, against the ref, against everything.'

Both sides had chances to win it in the second half, the best falling to France's Manuel Amoros, who hit the bar in the 83rd minute, but they remained deadlocked at 1–1 after ninety minutes.

Extra time saw momentum swing to the French, who scored twice in the first period through Mario Trésor and Alain Giresse. Two goals of such quality would have sent most opponents scuttling away with their heads in their hands, but not Germany. Throwing on half-fit captain Karl-Heinz Rummenigge was a final roll of the dice by coach Jupp Derwall, and it paid off when the sub scored in the 106th minute; two minutes later, the scores were level after a brilliant overhead kick from Klaus Fischer.

By the time the penalty shootout arrived — the first in finals history — the good vs. evil subplot was taken to its dramatic conclusion, with villain of the piece, Schumacher, playing a starring role. His saves from Didier Six and Maxime Bossis paved the way for Horst Hrubesch to put West Germany through to the final 5–4.

Coach Michel Hidalgo summed up the pain of defeat for France after the game:

> **They looked like a team of primary-school kids. They were all crying like children in the dressing rooms. We had to force them to undress and get into the showers, they were inconsolable.**

France 1 Brazil 1 (a.e.t), France won 4–3 on penalties
Quarterfinal, 21 June 1986, Estadio Jalisco, Guadalajara, Mexico

A match between the samba kings of Brazil and reigning European champions France was always going to promise much, but this quarterfinal was given added significance due to the two sides' heartbreaking exits four years earlier. Brazil had been sent packing by a Paolo Rossi–inspired Italy in the second round, while France were beaten on penalties by Germany in one of the most dramatic games in history. Only one team would get to exorcise their demons in the 45-degree Mexican heat.

Many of the faces were the same: Platini, Giresse, Tigana, Socrates, Zico, although France seemingly held the edge after a more impressive campaign en route to the quarters. But it was Brazil that landed the first blow as France seemed to struggle with the oppressive heat, Careca finishing off a wonderful move by Muller and Junior by blasting high past Joël Bats. France, driven by the promptings of Platini, gradually gained a foothold and, with only four minutes to half-time, Dominique Rocheteau's deflected cross flashed past Yannick Stopyra to find Platini at the far post. France's birthday boy had the simplest of side-foots to bring the game level.

That a game of such high-quality football didn't see another goal in regulation would normally be a disappointment, but the two sides played out a compelling second half, with chances going begging for both teams. With fifteen minutes remaining Branco was taken down in the box by Bats, and up stepped Zico, who had only entered the game two minutes earlier as a sub, to take the penalty. France's keeper guessed right and the Brazil penalty was soundly saved, but that was not the end of the goalkeeper-based drama. Brazil keeper Carlos clearly took out an onrushing Bruno Bellone, who was through on goal, but, just as in 1982 with Harald Schumacher, the referee saw nothing wrong with the mugging and waved play on.

'We all thought back to 1982,' said Manuel Amoros. 'But you play on, try to make it different this time.' If Socrates had slotted home in front of an open goal from the resulting Brazil break, then whatever small amount of justice that was still left in football would have died in the Mexican heat; fortunately karma kicked in and he spooned his shot over.

High drama followed the match into the penalty shootout: both Socrates and Platini missed their spot-kicks, while Bellone was karmically given a goal when it should have been disallowed (his shot bounced off the post and Carlos, then in). The deadlock was finally beaten when Júlio César hit the post and Luis Fernández converted for the victory.

In the aftermath the contrasting images told the story of the winners and losers: Platini hugged Fernández with a mixture of joy and relief, while Zico left the pitch close to tears, knowing his World Cup career was over. Journalist Hugh McIlvanney called it 'perhaps the most extraordinary contest in the entire history of the World Cup'.

Argentina 2 England 2 (a.e.t.), Argentina won 4–3 on penalties

Second Round, 30 June 1998, Stade Geoffroy-Guichard, Saint-Étienne, France

This second-round game was the first match between the bitter rivals since the 1986 'Hand of God' game, and tensions were running high: Maradona said 'the desire of the whole country is to beat England', while English newspaper *The Sun* showed their usual restraint by publishing a picture of Maradona's dodgy goal with the words '8pm Tonight. Payback time' on their front page. Although the public were being whipped up into a frenzy, the players kept their heads — with one notable exception — and partook in a modern-day classic.

The first forty-five minutes were played at a frenetic pace, momentum swinging one way and another before parity was restored at the end of the half. Argentina landed the first blow, Gabriel Batistuta becoming Argentina's all-time leading goalscorer when he dispatched a fifth-minute penalty after Diego Simeone was brought down in the box by David Seaman.

England weren't down for too long, however, as Michael Owen went down in a dive a South American would've been proud of and striker Alan Shearer finished from the penalty spot. England were in the ascendancy, with Owen's pace in particular scaring the bejesus out of the opposition defence.

In the sixteenth minute, the eighteen-year-old wunderkind introduced himself to the world with one of the best goals the tournament has ever seen. Running onto a David Beckham pass, the Liverpool forward turned on the afterburners and ran straight at defender Roberto Ayala, breezing past him and smacking his shot into Carlos Roa's far corner. (If you watch the footage again, you can see Paul Scholes running straight into the path of Owen's run, and he apparently makes a call to take the shot himself. Wisely, Owen declined the invitation and made World Cup history himself.)

Argentina calmly continued with their game plan and were rewarded in additional time at the end of the half when a well-worked free kick found Javier Zanetti alone in the box and he blasted past Seaman to even the score.

The turning point of the game came two minutes into the second half. David Beckham, grounded by a foul from Diego Simeone, flicked a boot up in retaliation and, although it hardly made contact, the Argentinean fell to the ground as if all the bones had been removed from his body. Referee Kim Milton Nielsen had no choice but to send 'Goldenballs' off, and England were left to fight it out with ten men for the rest of the game. Not that the battle was one-sided; England gave as good as they got in the second half and, while their backs were to the wall for most of the period, they did fashion the game's best chance: Sol Campbell's headed goal ten minutes from time was ruled out because of Shearer's foul on Roa.

Chances to score the golden goal in extra time were scarce, with England's Paul Ince and Tony Adams coming closest, but a shootout would ultimately decide the game. Both players in the second spot — Argentina's Crespo and England's Ince — missed their penalty, but the decisive kick lay at the feet of midfielder David Batty. On English TV, commentator Brian Moore asked Batty's club manager, Kevin Keegan, if Batty would score just as he stepped up; Keegan barely had time to answer 'yes' before Roa saved the spot-kick. Argentina booked a place in the quarterfinals against the Netherlands, and England suffered a penalty shootout heartache not for the last time.

7

THE WORLD CUP'S MOST STUNNING RESULTS

Another reason to do nothing but watch football during the four weeks of the World Cup is for the slim chance of seeing a good old-fashioned shocker.

In modern football, they don't happen too often; you might have to watch a lot of lopsided football games to reach this particular state of nirvana but, when you witness the shock result firsthand — the sheer elation of the winners and utter dejection of the losers — it makes it all worth it. (It's kind of the football equivalent of the prepubescent boy sitting through nearly an hour of *Trading Places* just to catch a glimpse of Jamie Lee Curtis's boobies.)

The history of the World Cup is littered with results that didn't go the favourites' way, but to qualify as a truly stunning result the game needs to have rocked the footballing world to its foundations. All of the following games qualify as the most rocking, shocking games ever seen.

USA 1 England 0
Group Stage, 29 June 1950, Estádio Raimundo Sampaio, Belo Horizonte, Brazil

England not only went into the game against the USA as favourites but, thanks to the mercurial talents of Stanley Matthews, Stan Mortensen and Tom Finney, they were tipped by many to win the whole tournament. The USA, in contrast, were a disparate bunch of amateurs and semi-pros who had been beaten 9–0 by Italy in a warm-up game.

The fixture was a mismatch of the highest order — bookies had the US at 500–1 to win — and England coach Walter Winterbottom rested his star, Matthews, for the game in expectation of sterner tests ahead. The game started true to form, with England running roughshod over the USA's defence (stats showed England had six scoring chances in the first twelve minutes), but they could not unlock it, due in no small part to USA defender Eddie McIlvenny, a naturalised Scot who had signed with Manchester United just before the tournament.

On thirty-seven minutes came the goal that shocked the world: Philadelphia schoolteacher Walter Bahr hit a speculative ball towards the England goal and up popped Haitian-born Brooklyn dishwasher Joe Gaetjens to nod the ball past Bert Williams.

The second half saw the expected onslaught from an increasingly frustrated England, but save after save from USA keeper Frank Borghi saw the Three Lions kept in check and earned the US the most historic and shocking of wins. After the match USA defender Harry Keough, a postal worker, said: 'Boy, I feel sorry for those bastards. How are they ever going to live down the fact we beat them?'

Back in the UK, the result was greeted much like England's shock 1882 test defeat to Australia from which the Ashes series was born; the *Daily Express* ran a report titled 'The death of English football' bordered in black. Fortunately, the England players didn't have to suffer the indignity of having their undercrackers burnt and put in an urn ...

Uruguay 2 Brazil 1
Final Pool, 16 July 1950, Maracanã Stadium, Rio de Janeiro, Brazil

To say Brazil were confident going into the World Cup's final game against Uruguay (the last game in the 'Final Pool' to decide the winner of a tournament without a 'final') would be an understatement. Powered by the attacking talents of Ademir, Jair and Zizinho, Brazil had swept all before them — in the final pool alone they had beaten Sweden 7–1 and Spain 6–1 — so Uruguay were not thought to pose much threat to their footballing coronation. Their officials thought as much, presenting the team with gold watches with 'For the World Champions' engraved on them a couple of days before the game, while the governor of the state of Rio hailed the team in a speech (at the Maracanã Stadium just before kick-off, no less):

> **You Brazilians, whom I consider victors of the tournament … you players who in less than a few hours will be acclaimed champions … you who have no equal in the terrestrial hemisphere … you who are superior to every other competitor … you whom I already salute as conquerors.**

The game began with Brazil playing like champions, sending wave after wave of attacks at the Uruguay goal; but for some last-ditch tackles and heroics from keeper Roque Máspoli, the game would have been over by half-time. All three of Brazil's famed attacking trio had clear-cut chances, but the match remained poised at 0–0 at the half.

Three minutes after the restart, Brazil finally broke Uruguay's defence. This time Ademir and Zizinho's forward movement left space for Friaça to put Brazil in the driving seat. Rather than dispirit *La Celeste*, the goal served to focus them; they saw more of the ball, and their attacks began to have a purpose previously lacking. Uruguay silenced the crowd in the 67th minute when Alcides Ghiggia's cross was put away by Juan Alberto Schiaffino.

'There was total silence,' said Máspoli. 'I knew then and there that the Brazilians were terrified of losing.'

A draw was still enough for Brazil to be champions, but a shift had taken place, and Uruguay looked the more likely to score. The winning goal came from Ghiggia, who took Brazil goalkeeper Moacir Barbosa by surprise at his near post. (Later the forward said he thought Barbosa was fooled into looking for the same move as the first goal, but instead of cross, this time he shot at goal.)

Again the crowd fell silent, and this time there was no answer. Uruguay had achieved the impossible and sent the home nation spiralling into a funereal-like stupor. The game became known as the '*Maracanãzo*', 'The Maracanã blow', and left a scar on Brazilian football, and its nation, that is still tender to this day.

West Germany 3 Hungary 2
World Cup Final, 4 July 1954, Wankdorf Stadium, Bern, Switzerland

Just as Brazil's eleven-goal thriller against Poland in 1938 introduced the footballing public to *jogo bonito*, so the 1954 World Cup Final established Germany's reputation as the team you should never bet against. No matter how many goals they are adrift by or how mismatched they are against an opponent, *die Mannschaft* always seem to find a way to win.

This assertion comes with the benefit of decades of hindsight, but in 1954, against hugely talented Hungary, who hadn't lost a game in four years, no-one was giving Germany much of a chance — especially as the Magyars had dismantled them 8–3 in the group stages. If you want an idea of how little a chance they were given in the final, consider the words of the German coach Sepp Herberger ahead of the game after daring to dream of a win:

> **It would be the greatest upset of the world championship. But we don't believe it, and we are making ready to hail as champions tomorrow that marvellous goal-scoring machine which is the great Hungarian team.**

Ten minutes into the match, Herberger's words rang true; Hungary were 2–0 up, and it looked like Germany had another shellacking on their hands. But the underdogs weren't rattled, and two minutes later they had pulled one back thanks to Max Morlock's outstretched leg. Eight minutes later Germany were, incredibly, on level terms, a Fritz Walter corner finding its way to Helmut Rahn who blasted home.

Germany's goals roused the dozing giant, and for the rest of the match Hungary rained attacks down on their opponents. If not for Toni Turek in Germany's goal, the Magyars would have romped to victory well before Rahn struck in the 84th-minute winner to complete the 'greatest upset'. Ferenc Puskás had one last chance to level the scores, but his goal four minutes from time was ruled out for offside — a decision that is still hotly disputed.

Several reasons for Germany's victory have been given over the years, from Puskás not being fully fit and Germany wearing studs in their boots to Fritz Walter's love of the rain and some dodgy doping by Germany's team doctor. But the biggest factor — Germany's 'never say die' attitude — is one that confounded not just Hungary, but many a future World Cup opponent too.

North Korea 1 Italy 0
Group Game, 19 July 1966, Ayresome Park, Middlesbrough, England

A little more than a decade removed from a controversial war, and still cloaked in Cold War secrecy, North Korea weren't particularly welcome at the 1966 World Cup. FIFA were more than a little embarrassed that the Asian nation had made the finals, so they chucked them up into a far corner of north-east England and banned national anthems from being played before the games so no-one had to listen the North Korean paean. But for Italy, facing the minnows of the tournament in their final group game would give them some much-needed practice for the more testing games to come later. They may have been in the minority, but Italy were happy to see North Korea. Or they were until the opening whistle blew.

North Korea had already surpassed most people's expectations by winning a point against Chile — and that draw gave them a glimmer of hope of progressing to the knockout stage with a win against two-time champions Italy. Their trump card was their speed and they used it to good effect against an ageing Italy defence, who were hindered even more when they went down to ten men after Bulgarelli limped off with a knee injury. Dancing past the Italy players almost at will, North Korea shocked the crowd in the 42nd minute by taking the lead through Pak Doo-Ik, who latched onto a speculative header forward and blasted past Enrico Albertosi. Despite having the second half to redress the balance, Italy had no response and were handed the most shocking of shock defeats.

Goalkeeper Ri Chan Myong, who played a blinder, summed up his teammates' attitude towards the game, where patriotism and love of their leader (and no small amount of brainwashing) gave fuel to their outstanding performance:

> Behind me the goal was small but behind the goal was our nation and if I conceded a goal the reputation of North Korea would fall. We would have failed in the task set us by the Great Leader. Therefore, I guarded the goal with my life.

It wasn't until the next day, when the Soviet Union beat Chile 2–1, that the fairytale/nightmare was complete: North Korea had made it to the quarterfinals and Italy were on their way home. Unsurprisingly, the *Azzurri* were greeted by a volley of rotten vegetables and, for the rest of the year, Italian players who took part in the game were serenaded with chants of 'Korea!' in every stadium they played.

West Germany 1 Austria 0
Group Game, 25 June 1982, Estadio El Molinón, Gijón, Spain

The match dubbed 'The Game of Shame' is probably the most disgraceful in all World Cup history. Algeria, the surprise team of Group Two after a 2–1 win over West Germany, stood on the verge of qualification thanks to a 3–2 win over Chile. But with the final game in the group being played a day later, Germany and Austria knew exactly what was needed for each to progress: a Germany win by one or two goals. Anything else and Algeria would go through.

What followed was an embarrassment of a football game, as the countries clearly entered into a gentleman's agreement to get the result both teams needed. Germany scored ten minutes into the match through Horst Hrubesch, and then both teams rolled the ball around the middle of the pitch for the next eighty minutes, hardly breaking a sweat.

Neither team made any pretence that the match was competitive, and the El Molinón crowd let their feelings known by whistling, jeering and waving bank notes at the two sides. Algeria made an official complaint to FIFA over the fixture, but their appeals fell on deaf ears, the governing body secretly happy that one of its powerhouse teams still remained despite being shithouse.

The German FA president was unrepentant, saying, 'There is no FIFA rule saying that teams cannot play as they wish,' although, as a direct result of the game, future final group games were organised to be played simultaneously. Leave it to the English press to sum up the game in typical pithy style, as one daily ran with the headline 'What a Load of Hrubesch'.

Cameroon 1 Argentina 0
Group Game, 8 June 1990, Stadio San Siro, Milan, Italy
Senegal 1 France 0
Group Game, 31 May 2002, World Cup Stadium, Seoul, South Korea

After the stunning performances of Cameroon and Senegal, reigning world champions now hope and pray they are not drawn against an African nation for the opening game of the tournament.

African dominance of the World Cup opener began with Cameroon's earth-shattering victory over champs Argentina in 1990. Although featuring a star-studded team including Diego Maradona, Claudio Caniggia and Abel Balbo, Argentina couldn't live with the athleticism, pace and roughhouse tactics of the Indomitable Lions. Weathering some early pressure, Cameroon soon became more comfortable with the game — and when they weren't, they just kicked their opponents until they were. (Caniggia was the most popular kicking post, victim of two red-card fouls in the game.) Halfway into the second half, François Omam-Biyik leapt, Michael Jordan–like, into the air and headed past Nery Pumpido into the Argentina goal. Despite a series of attacks in the final minutes, the nine men of Cameroon held on for a historic win.

Fast forward twelve years and it was the same old story. The current world and European champions were expected to brush aside unfancied Senegal in the first game of the 2002 tournament, but a jaded France were not at the races. Without talisman Zinedine Zidane, France were put to the sword by a vibrant and enthusiastic performance by Senegal. Papa Bouba Diop scored from an El Hadji Diouf cross and then promptly laid out his shirt on the ground and danced around it in celebration like it was a handbag in a Newcastle disco. France hit the woodwork through Thierry Henry but they couldn't find the goal they needed to avoid an opening-game humiliation.

On both occasions the Africans' wins were thought to be lucky, but both countries made their mark on the tournament: Cameroon became the first African nation to make it to the knockout stage and were unlucky not to make the semifinals, while Senegal made it out of their group and beat Sweden in the Round of 16 before going out to a golden goal against Turkey in the quarters.

South Korea 2 Italy 1 (a.e.t.), South Korea won with a golden goal
Second Round, 18 June 2002, World Cup Stadium, Daejeon, South Korea

South Korea were the darlings of the 2002 World Cup, seeing off three giants of European football en route to the semifinals, but no result was more shocking than their win over Italy in the second round. Buoyed by fanatic support and a coach (Guus Hiddink) who held an almost mystical sway over his squad, South Korea played out of their skins to see off an Italian side many were tipping for the top.

After Korea missed an early penalty, Christian Vieri put Italy into the lead with a strong header in the eighteenth minute — and that was the way the score stayed until two minutes from time, when a Christian Panucci error led to Seol Ki-Hyeon sweeping home the equaliser; Vieri blasting the simplest of crosses over an open goal a minute later only added insult to injury.

Buoyed by the comeback, South Korea kept up the pressure in extra time — but it was referee Byron Moreno who would take centre stage. First he ruled out a Damiano Tommasi goal for a marginal offside, and then he sent off Francesco Totti for diving when he was clearly fouled in the box. (Italy cried conspiracy, although nothing was ever proven.) To round off Italy's nightmare, Ahn Jung-Hwan — who missed the early penalty — rose to head home the golden goal winner four minutes from time.

In a delicious irony, Hwan played his football in Italy, although prickly Perugia president Luciano Gaucci bitterly proclaimed Hwan had played his last game for the club: 'I have no intention of paying a salary to someone who has ruined Italian football.'

8

THE WORLD CUP'S
BIGGEST SHOCKERS

One of football's finest qualities is its ability to surprise its fans. Some of the most astonishing results in the history of the tournament have already been covered in the previous chapter. But over its history the World Cup has witnessed several shocking moments that have had very little to do with a team of eleven men trying to score more goals than their opponents: dodgy dictators have used the tournament to enhance their own prestige, loose-lipped coaches have caused international incidents, a player has had his life destroyed for letting in a goal, and, in the most extreme case, a player has been shot for scoring in his own net. And that's before we even get to all the kicking, punching, spitting and head-butting that goes on between rival players, the best of which get their very own names, like the 'Battle of Santiago' or the 'Battle of Bern'.

However, if there's one shocking World Cup event that sums up the high-stakes, pressure-cooker atmosphere that can destroy even the most experienced of performers, it has to be the earth-shattering penalty miss in the 1994 World Cup. With the eyes of the world watching, the stage was set for the protagonist to hit the back of the net and wheel away to be hailed by their adoring public. But a World Cup penalty kick can be a cruel mistress and the terrible miss left the taker humiliated in front of billions of fans, career in tatters. Certainly Diana Ross never kicked another ball after her opening ceremony spot-kick debacle ...

Under the shadows of dictators

Anyone who says politics and football don't mix obviously knows nothing about either. Global sporting events have been, and continue to be, used by governments to create a 'feel-good factor' and distract the masses from any number of social problems that are afflicting their nation. The World Cup is a prime example. Looking at it in solely monetary terms, organisers have bent over backwards to host the tournament, from agreeing to pay all participants' costs (Uruguay in 1930) and overlooking a national disaster (Chile ploughed on in 1962 despite a devastating earthquake) to mortgaging their homes (US Federation lawyer Scott LeTellier put up his house to raise cash in '94) and violating several human rights laws (the latest scandal involves immigrant workers in 2022 host nation Qatar).

Any leader worth their salt knows that associating themselves with the tournament will give them the kind of political capital money can't buy, and throughout the World Cup's history some of the world's most brutal dictators have benefitted from cosying up to FIFA's showcase event.

Italy's Benito Mussolini was the first to harness the power of the World Cup for political gain, using the finals as a propaganda tool to unite his nation. Il Duce's influence was everywhere — he even commissioned a second cup, the Coppa del Duce, which was six times the size of the Jules Rimet trophy, for the teams to compete for — and was said to have 'requested' that Italy coach Victor Pozzo select only Fascist party members to the national team.

Where Mussolini's influence was at its most nefarious was in the selection of 'friendly' referees. The controversial ref who took charge of Italy's games against Spain was immediately suspended upon returning home to Switzerland, and it emerged that Swedish official Ivan Elkind, who was in charge of the Italy vs. Austria semifinal, had dinner with Mussolini the previous night to talk 'tactics'. The Italian leader then made the startling request to have Elkind ref the final against Czechoslovakia (and what Il

Duce wants, Il Duce gets) and the Swede was introduced to fascist officials before the game. The phrase 'the result was never in doubt' has never been so true.

Europe's other fascist dictator of the time, Germany's Adolf Hitler, had just as powerful a hand over World Cup proceedings. He wasn't a football fan — he was said to have attended only one game, the 2–0 defeat to Norway in the 1936 Olympics, and left it early in a rage — but he was well aware of its power. In the 1938 finals in France he ordered players from annexed Austria to play for the 'Greater Germany' team, and there were protests both inside and outside the grounds Germany were playing in by Jewish and anti-fascist groups. Fascist salutes were the norm during the national anthems of both Germany and Italy, although the opposition teams resisted the request to join them in striking the pose.

Mussolini was still at it in '38 too, ordering his team to play in 'fascist party' black when their kits clashed with France (although Italian FA head General Vaccaro stood up to Il Duce by telling him the *Azzurri* would never play in that colour again), then sending a sinister telegram reading *'Vincere o morire'* — loosely translated as 'win or die' — to his team before the final. No pressure then, lads …

Nearly forty years later, President Mobutu of Zaire also utilised the fascist blueprint when his country took part in the 1974 finals in Germany. As the first black African nation to qualify for the finals, Mobutu used the team to promote 'black pride' as part of his country's anti-West rebranding. Players were promised cars, holidays and houses if they performed well — but it soon became obvious the rewards would never arrive, especially when results didn't go The Leopards' way. Defender Mwepu Ilunga said:

Mobutu was like a father to us before we went. We thought that we would all come back millionaires. But we got back home with nothing in our pockets. Now I live like a tramp.

Events took a frightening turn before Zaire's final game against Brazil. The team had lost 9–0 to Yugoslavia after threatening to strike over non-payment of wages, but it was Mobutu who was the one with an ultimatum before the game against the South Americans: lose by more than three goals against Brazil, and you will never see Zaire or your families again. Thankfully, Zaire lost 3–0 and the players returned home safely.

Political interference is just as prevalent in the modern game. While 1978 was the last time a totalitarian regime has held the finals — Argentinean General Jorge Videla cleverly used the finals to whip up support at home and legitimise his brutal military junta to the world — politics is still front and centre in world football. However, the 'dictator' role has now shifted from heads of state to within FIFA itself, as President Sepp Blatter sits as a modern-day despot overseeing a fundamentally corrupt and poisonous association. It says much about the magic and allure of the World Cup that, despite knowing its leaders are rotten to the core, fans still can't get enough of the greatest football tournament in the world.

Moacir Barbosa, 1950

When heavily favoured Brazil lost the 1950 World Cup Final to Uruguay, a nation in mourning needed a scapegoat. Enter goalkeeper Moacir Barbosa. The twenty-nine-year-old keeper was quickly blamed for the most shocking defeat in the history of the game, not least because he was caught out at the near post by Uruguay's Alcides Ghiggia for the winning goal. No matter that Barbosa was Brazil's greatest-ever goalkeeper, with a career spanning more than two decades; he was the man every Brazilian blamed for the loss and it destroyed his career and affected the rest of his life.

Barbosa played only one more game for the national team and later worked as a cleaner at the Maracanã, the scene of his footballing 'crime'. Legend has it that when the goalposts were replaced in the early '60s, he took them home and burned them in his garden.

While the bonfire may have exorcised some personal ghosts, it didn't stop others from reminding him of his failure; for years people spat on him in public and would avoid walking past him in the street. He was blocked from being a commentator on Brazil games and the ultimate insult came in 1994, when he was refused entry to the Brazil training camp; the team believed he was bad luck ahead of that year's finals.

Barbosa died in relative poverty in 2000, and in an interview just before his death, he explained how the events of that fateful day haunted him for the rest of his life: 'The maximum punishment in Brazil is thirty years' imprisonment, but I have been paying for something that I'm not even responsible for fifty years.'

The Battle of Bern, 1954

The 1954 quarterfinal between Brazil and Hungary featured two of the most talented teams of their generation. Brazil might have been reeling from their final defeat four years earlier, but they still played with a flair and creativity that made them the envy of most nations. Hungary had one of the greatest football teams ever assembled: the Magical Magyars featured the talents of Ferenc Puskás, Sándor Kocsis, Jósef Bozsik and Nándor Hidegkuti, and they were on a four-year undefeated streak. So it was shocking on many levels that their match was to descend into such violence that it was to be forever known as the 'Battle of Bern'. By the time the final whistle was blown by English referee Arthur Ellis, three players had been sent off, with forty-two free kicks and two penalties awarded.

Clearly not able to live with Hungary in a football sense — they went 2–0 down after just seven minutes — Brazil started to lay into their opponents with some tasty challenges, and

Hungary responded in kind. In the second half Ellis awarded a hotly disputed penalty to Hungary, and the game went to shit. Five minutes later, Bozsik and Nílton Santos were sent off for fisticuffs, with officials and police entering the field to get involved too. The rough tackles kept coming until the ref had no choice but to red card Brazil's Humberto Tozzi after a shocking foul on Gyula Lóránt.

Scenes at the final whistle went from bad to worse, as players, officials, police and media all became involved in an on-pitch rumble that continued as the teams made their way back to the dressing rooms. Italian newspaper *Corriere della Sera* reported that Puskás, who was injured and didn't play in the game, made his way down the tunnel afterwards and 'struck the Brazilian centre-half Pinheiro in the face with a bottle as he was entering the dressing rooms, causing a wound eight centimetres long' (although other witnesses have said it was a spectator and not the 'Galloping Major'). In retaliation, Brazil went back to their changing rooms to get some bottles and launched an attack on Hungary's dressing room, leaving one player unconscious and the coach badly cut. (Oh, and for the three of you reading on to find out the result of the match, Hungary won 4–2.)

As a (vaguely) interesting aside, referee Ellis would go on to enjoy fame as 'referee' for popular UK TV game show *It's a Knockout*, something the 'Battle of Bern' surely helped him prepare for.

The Battle of Santiago, 1962

While the venue for the 'Battle of Bern' gives off a distinct vibe of Swiss neutrality (who battles in Switzerland anyway?), the 'Battle of Santiago' evokes images of fiery Latinos hell-bent on causing carnage against a mortal enemy. Which pretty much accurately sums up the events of the game between Chile and Italy played in the host nation's capital in 1962.

The two countries were hardly on good terms after a series of disparaging articles were written about Chilean life in Italian newspapers. One piece read: 'Chile is a foul country afflicted by every evil — undernourishment, illiteracy, alcoholism, open prostitution and general misery.' Italy tried to diffuse the tension before the game by offering their opponents carnations — but they were refused, and it took twelve seconds before referee Ken Aston had to rule on the first foul of the game. Eight minutes in and there was already a sending off, Italy's Giorgio Ferrini red carded for retaliating after being kicked from behind by Chile forward Landa. Ferrini refused to go, and it took ten minutes to get the agitated player off the pitch so play could resume.

One of the major protagonists was Chile's Leonel Sánchez, who could actually play a bit (he was joint top scorer, with four goals in the tournament). He floored Mario David with a left hook after being persistently kicked by the Italian, only for David to aim a flying kick at his neck later in the game and get sent off himself. Sánchez also broke the nose of Italy captain Humberto Maschio right in front of the linesman, but the assault went unpunished.

The teams were so caught up in petty squabbles and revenge that they forgot about trying to score. Armed police had to come on the field twice, the ref was constantly jostled by players and he nearly abandoned the game but for fear of what the Chilean crowd might do to him if he did. As it turned out, he needed an armed guard to take him off the pitch: 'It was me against twenty-two. The game was uncontrollable.'

Watching the match now in grainy black and white on YouTube is pretty funny, as Benny Hill–esque characters run around kicking and punching each other at every turn, but at the time the events were scandalous. Commentator David Coleman, introducing it on tape delay to the English audience, summed up the mood at the time with this solemn introduction:

“Good evening. The game you are about to see is the most stupid, appalling, disgusting and disgraceful exhibition of football possibly in the history of the game. Chile vs. Italy: this is the first time the two countries have met; we hope it will be the last. The national motto of Chile reads: 'By reason or by force.' Today the Chileans were prepared to be reasonable, the Italians only used force and the result was a disaster for the World Cup.”

England, Argentina and the 'animals' incident, 1966

“We still have to produce our best, and this is not possible until we meet the right type of opponents, and that is a team that comes out to play football and not act as animals.”

England coach Alf Ramsey was known for his contempt of all things foreign — people, food, countries — but by announcing that his opponents in the 1966 quarterfinal, Argentina, were nothing more than 'animals', he unwittingly became involved in what journalist Hugh McIlvanney called 'not so much a football match as an international incident'.

There was no love lost between the two nations, and on the football pitch in the mid-'60s they were both known for being able to put it about a bit as well as playing decent football. Argentina had already earned a FIFA warning for rough play against West Germany, and England's Nobby Stiles was walking a disciplinary tightrope after an atrocious tackle against France, but they took foul play to a new level in the infamous quarterfinal.

Almost from the off, Argentina were involved in a variety of spitting, kicking, hair-pulling, pube-twisting and eye-poking antics (one of those I made up) in an effort to put the English off their game. *Albiceleste* captain Antonio Rattín felt that German referee Rudolf Kreitlein was biased against his team, and after he complained one too many times he was sent off. It was a pretty harsh decision, especially considering Kreitlein didn't actually understand what Rattín had said to him, later calling it a dismissal for 'the look on his face' and 'violence of the tongue'. Rattín refused to walk and it took ten minutes for him to leave the pitch; he later claimed that he was asking for an interpreter. He stewed on the red carpet laid out for the queen and is alleged to have given a one-fingered salute in her direction. In fact, Argentina had their panties so tightly in a bunch that when a ball boy ran onto the pitch to celebrate Geoff Hurst's 77th-minute goal, defender Oscar Más gave him a clump around the ear and sent him on his way!

England, and Ramsey in particular, were not without fault in the controversy though. The England coach had primed his side for the battle ahead by stating in his pre-match speech: 'Gentlemen, you know what kind of a match you will have on your hands today.' England captain Bobby Moore said, 'We accepted in our guts it was going to be hard. Maybe brutal.'

But Rattín's assertion that the referee was more lenient towards England does seem to hold some water when watching the game back, as he ignored several strong challenges by Cohen and Stiles in the first half. In fact, the official foul count ended at England 33, Argentina 19.

At the end of the game, Ramsey refused to let his team swap shirts with their opponents. (Remember the iconic image of George Cohen and Alberto Gonzalez trying to swap a shirt, with Ramsey stopping them? Ramsey said: 'George, you are not swapping shirts with people like this'; the Argentinean then walked away and swapped with Ray Wilson instead.)

Ramsey's 'animals' comment came in a post-match interview and, although he would later retract his statement, the Argentinean press had already run with stories that the England manager was calling all of their countrymen animals; 'Shameful English Insult' was just one of the many headlines. The reverberations from the incident continued through match-ups in the 1986 and 1998 finals, and the 1966 quarterfinal remains at the heart of one of the most heated rivalries in football.

Argentina 6 Peru 0, 1978

Proving that a football match is fixed is a difficult undertaking, but if a list was compiled of World Cup matches that were 'heavily influenced by outside forces in order to obtain a favourable result', then Argentina's game against Peru in 1978 would be at the top of the page.

Hosts Argentina had the near-impossible task of having to win by at least four goals against their South American neighbours in order to make it to the World Cup Final, in a tournament as important for brutal leader General Videla's prestige and ego as it was for the players. So when the *albiceleste* ended the game as 6–0 winners, talk of dodgy dealings surfaced almost immediately. A little bit of delving revealed that Peru's keeper, Ramón Quiroga, was born in Argentina — and their reserve keeper Manzo admitted in a drunken conversation that the fix was for real, before retracting his statement the next day.

Rumours continued to rumble on: in 1986 *The Sunday Times* published an article by journalist María Laura Avignolo that said a deal had been struck whereby a shipment of 35,000 tons of grain and a credit line of US$50 million was given to Peru soon after the match; an unnamed Peru player said their starting eleven were paid US$20,000 in cash by an Argentinean official after the game; and reserve midfielder Raúl Gorriti told John Spurling in his book *Death or Glory: The Dark History of the World Cup* that General Videla had made an appearance in the Peruvian dressing room before the match, asking 'the Latin brothers to stick together' and having a few quiet words with their coach.

Like the best conspiracy theories, the fix has never been proven. But if a murderous military dictator turned up to the dressing room and made veiled threats about what would happen if you didn't lose the game, I'd be less inclined to play my hardest too ...

Harald Schumacher touches up Patrick Battiston, 1982

If the 'Battle of Santiago' is the black-and-white era's most brutal World Cup moment, West Germany goalkeeper Harald Schumacher's mugging of France's Patrick Battiston in the 1982 semifinal is probably the most violent act of the colour era (although the word 'violent' doesn't go anywhere near adequately describing the sickening events of that night in Seville).

Early in the second half Battiston was played through on goal by a brilliant pass from Michel Platini and, as Schumacher rushed out, the Frenchman met the ball first only to knock his shot wide. Then, rather than pulling out of the challenge (and he had time to do so), Schumacher followed through by jumping into the defenceless attacker, chest high.

'I knew the goalkeeper would come for it,' said Battiston of the clash.

> **I saw him coming but it was too late. I was desperate to score and that's why I didn't pull out. That's why it was such a big collision. I don't remember much more about it.**

It was a sickening clash and Battiston lay motionless on the ground for several minutes; it turned out he had cracked some vertebrae and had two teeth knocked out. Dutch referee Charles Corver didn't deem the collision worthy of even a yellow card, when it was clearly a straight red offence. (Corver would later say his view of the incident was obscured and when he asked his linesman if it was a foul, he was told the clash was not intentional.) But what really galled those watching was Schumacher's reaction afterwards. As a frantic crowd gathered around the Frenchman —

Platini thought he was dead — and medics administered oxygen, the German stood by the ball waiting to take the goal-kick, waving for play to continue as if to imply Battiston was faking it. There was not a word of apology or any sign of remorse. (Schumacher later said he was staying away from the rest of the gathering France team, for fear of copping a beat-down.)

After escaping punishment, Schumacher went on to be the hero of the resulting penalty shootout, saving two French spot-kicks to send Germany through to the final. The goalkeeper, and Germany by default, became public enemy number one, leading to a large groundswell of support for Italy in the final.

Looking back on the event years later, Schumacher was hardly repentant — but he did admit he would have done one thing differently.

> If I was still keeping goal today, I'd have come off my line in exactly the same way. What I would do differently nowadays is this: my behaviour while he was being treated and after the match was just not acceptable.

Theft of the Jules Rimet Trophy in Brazil, 1983

The iconic Jules Rimet Trophy — awarded to every World Cup winner from 1930 until 1970, when it was permanently handed over to Brazil after they won their third title — was stolen on two occasions: once in 1966, and again in 1983. The first time was in England, causing a scandal of such magnitude that Abrain Tebel of the Brazilian Sports Confederation told *The Times*: 'This shameful theft would never have happened in Brazil. Even Brazilian thieves love football and would never have committed such a sacrilegious crime.' As for the second theft, take a wild guess about where that took place.

Housed at the Brazilian Football Federation in Rio de Janeiro, the trophy was stolen by thieves who trussed up the nightwatchman and cleverly bypassed the display cabinet's bulletproof glass by prying off the wooden back. Pleas were made for the trophy's safe return, and even Pelé was involved in an appeal (although, knowing his crappy prediction skills, he probably told people not to worry and that the trophy would be safely returned).

But by the time three Brazilians and an Argentinean were arrested for the theft, police believed the trophy had already been melted down (although one rumour is that the cup was stolen to order for a fanatical collector). Brazil's carelessness with the original trophy led to heightened security around the new World Cup; three-time winners are now not allowed to keep the trophy and the winner has to return the original to FIFA in return for a replica for display purposes.

The Hand of God, 1986

The term 'Hand of God' is said to derive from medieval times when painting God in human form was seen as unacceptable, so a solitary hand was often used to illustrate his influence or intervention in an event on earth. The phrase is now more popularly used to describe what is the single most controversial incident in World Cup history: Diego Maradona's first goal against England in the 1986 quarterfinal, as the man himself described it as 'a little of the hand of God and a little of the head of Maradona'.

The 'goal' is etched in every football fan's memory; as El Diego launched an attack on the England goal early in the second half, defender Steve Hodge lobbed a high back pass towards goalkeeper Peter Shilton. Maradona continued his run into the box, but there looked to be little danger the 165-centimetre Argentinean would be able to able to out-jump 185-centimetre Shilton to the ball. But he did, a combination of the English keeper displaying the leaping ability of an elephant with a full stomach and Maradona surreptitiously using his hand.

Maradona's reaction to the goal was a bit of a giveaway, as

he first looked around guiltily to see if he'd gotten away with the blatant handball. When he realised the goal had been given by referee Ali Bin Nasser, he quickly gestured to his teammates to join him, telling them to celebrate with him in order to make the goal look more legit.

The goal shocked England to the core; they were unable to comprehend how the referee had missed such an obvious transgression. In the immediate aftermath, Maradona scored a sublime second by running through the England defence as if they were statues and, despite a late goal from Gary Lineker making the score 2–1, Argentina won thanks to goals that exhibited both sides of their tortured genius.

The English and Argentinean response to Maradona's antics highlighted the cultural differences between the two nations when it came to an act of footballing subterfuge. The English public immediately condemned the act as the ultimate in unsportsmanlike behaviour and branded Maradona a cheat; it conveniently allowed them to forget England went on to concede the greatest goal ever scored, and that they were second best on the day. In Argentina, Maradona's act was hailed not as cheating, but as cheekiness, harking back to the *pibe* in Argentinean folklore who uses his street smarts and cunning to get one over on the establishment.

It's also worth noting the role the Falklands conflict played in shaping events, both in the media and in Maradona's own mind. Argentinean newspaper *Cronica* ran with the headline 'Malvinas 2 England 1' and said of the win, 'We beat the pirates with Maradona and a little hand … This time the queen didn't have Reagan … God save Argentina', while Maradona admitted in his autobiography *El Diego*:

> **This was revenge. It was like recovering a little bit of the Malvinas. In the pre-match interviews we had all said that football and politics shouldn't be confused, but that was a lie. We did nothing but think about that.**

Rijkaard and Völler's spat, 1990

Netherlands midfielder Frank Rijkaard single-handedly put the 'spat' into World Cup tussles with his saliva-inspired effort to add a bit of volume to German Rudi Völler's locks. The Netherlands and Germany were old enemies, both on and off the pitch, and the enmity was still alive and kicking in this second-round game at the San Siro in Milan. Twenty-one minutes into the match, Rijkaard slid in on Völler and the German went down as if shot by a sniper. The Dutchman was given a yellow card but, as he jogged past his German antagonist, he matter-of-factly spat into his fluffy mullet. The two immediately clashed again, both pointing and making the universal lobster gesture, signifying 'You're all mouth and no trousers', and as Völler pointed out the spit in his hair to the referee, he was booked as well. (Völler's mullet had a bit of the *Coming to America* Jheri curl about it, and the ref may have thought the spit was just Soul Glo).

The feud bubbled away until Völler clashed with the Netherlands keeper and Rijkaard jumped in again. As the referee reached for his pocket to send both players off, Rijkaard is caught on camera coughing up a big greenie in preparation and, as the battling duo jogged off towards the tunnel, the Dutchman launched it into Völler's hair, with a subsequent camera shot showing the coagulated throat syrup dangling from the German's mullet. Rijkaard ran off with the classic schoolboy 'it wasn't me, Sir' look, while Völler was left to inspect the mess in his palm.

Rijkaard apologised to Völler for the incident a few months later, and the two even starred in a TV commercial a couple of years later to show there were no hard feelings. Völler told *FourFourTwo*:

> **A Dutch butter company came up with the idea of a public reconciliation under the slogan 'Everything in Butter Again', which is a German proverb meaning that everything is okay again.**

Diana Ross's penalty miss, 1994

The 1994 World Cup finals were bookended by two of the worst penalty misses ever seen. Roberto Baggio's penalty shootout blast into Row Z will be remembered as the kick that handed the World Cup to Brazil, but Diana Ross's spot-kick miss in the opening ceremony will go down as one of the biggest crimes ever perpetrated against football.

Events at the grand opening at Chicago's Soldier Field didn't get off to the best of starts when singer Jon Secada broke his collarbone in a fall after the trapdoor he was set to emerge from jammed. Deciding not to wuss out in front of a billion-plus TV audience, he continued singing with just his head and shoulders poking out onto the stage, like a sequinned sewer worker belting a tune out of a manhole. It was a portent for what was about to befall Ross.

Given the assignment of scoring a penalty kick as part of the opening ceremony show, the former Supreme strode up with plenty of confidence, resplendent in a two-piece red suit and happily waving to the crowd. The goal should have been academic; no more than 6 metres out from goal, Ross was aided by the fact that there were kids crouching down either side of her to create a natural 'bumper bowling lane' to shoot down. If you look at the footage in slow motion, you can see how bad the miss is. The final child is placed to create a natural angle towards the goal and to ensure Ross cannot fail to score if she misses any human barrier; but she actually lifts the ball over the child, who ducks at the last second, and the shot spoons wide.

The cherry on top was the collapsing goalposts, designed to fall apart in a 'chain reaction' when the ball hit the back of the net. The ball went wide, the keeper dived almost out of pity and the posts blew apart, presumably now from the collective intake of breath coming from fans in attendance. Ross's blunder wasn't missed by the English press, who highlighted her soccerball deficiency with the headlines 'Miss Diana Ross' and 'Ain't No Goalposts Wide Enough'.

The murder of Andrés Escobar, 1994

When news broke that Colombia defender Andrés Escobar had been shot and killed in Medellín just a few days after playing in the World Cup finals, the entire football family went into mourning. How could a player who was known as '*El Caballero*' ('The Gentleman'), one of the most highly respected members of the national team, wind up murdered outside a nightclub?

Reports soon emerged that the twenty-seven-year-old had been killed because of his own goal against the USA two weeks earlier, a result that condemned Colombia to crashing out of the finals at the group stage. Escobar's killer allegedly shouted 'Goal!' every time he pulled the trigger, while some stories painted him as the victim of angry cartel bosses who had put substantial sums on Colombia to win the World Cup.

Colombia's '94 World Cup campaign was a disaster from the off. Given the dreaded Pelé nod of approval as the pre-tournament favourites after beating Argentina 5–0 in a qualifier, the team began with a defeat to Romania. Before their second game against the USA, two out-of-form players received calls telling them their houses would be burnt down if they played. Under intense pressure to perform, the Colombians lost 2–1, Escobar's own goal from a John Harkes cross proving the fatal wound. Ever the optimist, Escobar fronted the press afterwards and told them: 'This is football. Life goes on.'

The players were encouraged by coach Pacho Maturana to stay in the US and do some sightseeing after their early exit, but Escobar decided to return home — and it was while at a nightclub in his hometown of Medellín on 2 July 1994 that the young defender was shot and killed. Early stories said Escobar had been taunted about his own goal by some local gangsters, the Gallon brothers, and when he uncharacteristically responded, he was shot by their driver, Humberto Munoz. One report said it was an enraged fan exacting revenge for the defeat, while another said it was due to him approaching a woman in the club (although that seems strange, as he was out with his fiancée on the night in question). The reality is that no-one will ever know the real reason the defender was shot; his murder was just one of thousands that took place in Colombia during the notorious '90s.

Escobar's memory lives on in his home country. One hundred thousand people lined the streets for his funeral, and his name is still chanted from the terraces of his club, Atlético Nacional, where a statue stands in tribute of the man cut down in the prime of his life.

Zidane's head-butt, 2006

France's Zinedine Zidane had previous form in the World Cup nutter stakes — he was sent off in a 1998 group game for stamping on an opponent and was suspended for two games — but no-one could have predicted his astonishing head-butt on Italian Marco Materazzi with just ten minutes to go in the final of the 2006 World Cup. The image of a coiled-up Zidane launching himself into a crumpling Materazzi has already entered tournament folklore, and the Frenchman's decision to react rather than walk away saw the final game of his career morph from a fairytale to a nightmare in a split second.

The 2006 tournament had been a dream up to that point for Zidane, a hero coming out of retirement to lead his band of ageing brothers to one last hurrah; his performances were inspirational, especially in the 1–0 wins over Brazil and Portugal in the knockout stages. In the final against Italy, his seventh-minute penalty gave *Les Bleus* the lead before a Materazzi header levelled things up, and the teams remained deadlocked until deep into extra time.

It was then Zidane lost his head. With eight minutes to go, a seemingly innocuous challenge — the Italian had his arms loosely around the Frenchman from behind, tugging his shirt — sparked a war of words that saw Zidane snap, spinning around to launch himself headfirst and butt Materazzi to the floor.

As Argentinean referee Hector Elizondo arrived on the scene there was little doubt about the colour of the card Zidane would be shown. 'Zizou' walked dejectedly off the field, within touching distance of the trophy he had hoped to hold aloft. France held out for penalties but Italy triumphed in the shootout, Materazzi leading the celebrations around the Olympic Stadium pitch.

In the immediate aftermath, the internet was awash with what Materazzi must have said to provoke such a reaction from Zidane. The Frenchman's Muslim background led to talk of the Italian calling him a terrorist, although that was quickly discounted after both parties said it was over insults aimed at Zidane's family.

Over time, the events became clearer. Just before the butt, when Materazzi was pulling his shirt, Zidane said: 'If you want my shirt that badly, I will give it to you at the end of the match.' To which the Italian replied, 'I prefer the whore that is your sister.' After several comments aimed at him during the game by the Italian players, this was the final insult and Zidane decided to take it back to the Marseille of his youth and administer a little street justice. It was a shocking act — who head-butts someone in the chest? — and robbed one of the greatest footballing careers of a fitting finale.

Old wounds from the events of that night in Berlin remain raw. Materazzi said in a 2010 interview that he was still upset about the butt and he had yet to receive an apology from Zidane, to which the Frenchman replied that he would rather die than apologise for his actions.

'More than once they insulted my mother and I never responded,' Zidane told *El País*.

> **And [then] it happened. To apologise for this? No. If I ask him forgiveness, I lack respect for myself and for all those I hold dear with my heart. I apologise to football, to the fans, to the team but to him I cannot. Never, never. It would dishonour me. I'd rather die.**

Just so we're clear, that's a no then, Zinedine?

9

WORLD CUP CONSPIRACY THEORIES

It should come as no surprise that the World Cup has had its fair share of conspiracy theories, especially seeing as the tournament was founded on skullduggery and subterfuge. After all, there wouldn't have even been a World Cup finals if not for those unscrupulous turn-of-the-century professionals playing for their amateur national Olympic teams on the quiet.

Ropy referees

Early World Cup conspiracies centred mostly around the selection of 'sympathetic' refs to aid certain teams' progression, most notably in 1934 when Italian dictator Benito Mussolini took it upon himself to personally pick the men in black for the majority of Italy's games (which was pretty good of him, seeing as he was quite busy beating up and killing several thousands of his countrymen at the time). Not worried about concealing their intentions, the referees' decisions were so prejudiced towards Italy that one was subsequently banned and another was accused of such bias that he might as well have been wearing an Italy jersey: 'The referee even played for them,' said one Austrian player after his team suffered a 1–0 defeat in the semifinal. 'When I passed the ball out to the right wing, one of our players ran for it and the referee headed it back to the Italians.'

Dodgy doping

As a predominantly modern concept, conspiracy theories didn't really take hold in the World Cup until the early '50s. It all kicked off in the 1954 final, with the accusation that Germany were 'juiced up' for their 3–2 victory against seemingly unbeatable Hungary. Magyar captain Ferenc Puskás raised a few eyebrows when he said he saw several Germany players throwing up in the changing rooms after the match, and suspicions were raised further when many team members came down with jaundice the following week. After a stadium worker revealed he had found syringes in the changing room after the game, team doctor Franz Loogen was forced to admit that the players had been injected with vitamin C, and that the jaundice was caused by him using a dirty needle.

However, a 500-page study published in 2013 by the Humboldt University in Berlin and the University of Münster claimed that players were injected with the methamphetamine Pervitin, a drug nicknamed 'Panzer chocolate' as it was given to German soldiers fighting in WWII. The study, entitled 'Doping in Germany from 1950 to Today', stated the injections were part of a systematic doping program backed by the West German government that went on undetected for decades across several professional and Olympic sports. (The study also said several Germany players in the 1966 World Cup team were taking the stimulant ephedrine.)

Germany players weren't the only ones to be doped, with or without their knowledge. England keeper Gordon Banks first thought the dicky tummy that caused him to miss the 1970 quarterfinal against West Germany was the result of a dodgy Mexican beer — but rumours later swirled that the spiking was by Brazil sympathisers who wanted to ensure the exit of England, the only team they saw as a threat.

If that was true, then karma bit back at Italia 90 when Brazil's Branco claimed he was drugged by an Argentinean trainer who handed him a bottle during a pause in play in their second-round match. He said he felt 'dizzy and uncoordinated' for the rest of the game and he failed to pick up Diego Maradona, leading to the winning Argentina goal.

Nothing could be proven until December 2004, when Diego Maradona said in an interview that the Brazilian's claims were correct; the water contained Rohypnol, the 'date rape' drug, although the Argentinean FA later countered by saying 'Maradona was not in control of his senses' (which is a fair point). There was added intrigue when an Argentinean newspaper asked the *albiceleste* boss at the time, Carlos Bilardo, if it happened and he replied, 'I'm not saying it didn't happen' (while probably winking and mouthing 'It happened').

Video evidence seems to back up Branco's claims, as you can clearly see an Argentinean player taking a swig from a green bottle before immediately spitting out the liquid after being shouted at by the trainer. Instead he drinks from a clear bottle and the green bottle is then passed on to Branco, who takes a big gulp and begins his descent into wooziness and bad defending.

Konspiration 58

If tales of doping and cover-ups aren't too hard to believe in this day and age, then the story surrounding the 'fake' 1958 World Cup is a little harder to swallow. Released in 2002, Swedish documentary *Konspiration 58* claimed the finals in Sweden didn't actually take place and that the footage was forged by Swedish and American TV companies as part of a Cold War strategy to test how far people would believe propaganda on television.

The show claimed that Sweden did not have the money or know-how to host such a big event, and 'experts' looked at shadows on the ground around the players to prove the matches couldn't possibly been played in Sweden; even UEFA suit Lennart Johansson was filmed giving his opinion on events. At the end of the compelling show, producers revealed it to be a mockumentary warning about the pitfalls of media manipulation, but many people took the show at face value and continue to believe the fabricated evidence.

The fixes

On the madness scale, closely following those who don't believe the World Cup was played in Scandinavia in 1958 is ex-FIFA president João Havelange, who gave an interview saying both the 1966 and 1974 World Cups were fixed. The then-ninety-two-year-old Brazilian told *Folha de Sao Paulo* in 2008 that England and Germany fixed the results of their home World Cups in order to break the dominance of Brazil.

> "We were the best team in the world, and had the same team that won the World Cup in 1962 in Chile and 1970 in Mexico, but it was planned for the host countries to win ... [In 1966] what was the final? England vs. Germany. Why were there only German and English referees in my games? The same happened in 1974, in Germany. Do you not think that is strange? And I ask you, did England ever become a champion again, or did it win anything? No."

Havelange — whose photographic memory didn't stretch to remembering that the Brazil team in 1974 was pants — would know a thing a thing or two about the shady side of the World Cup, having been involved in his own controversy over the hosting of the 1986 finals. When Colombia announced they had to pull out as hosts due to financial difficulties, Mexico, the USA and Canada made bids to hold the tournament, with the venerable Henry Kissinger adding weight to the USA presentation at a meeting in Stockholm in May 1983. Not even formally considering the American bid, the FIFA World Cup committee announced the 1986 finals would go to Mexico, despite the fact that the nation was having severe financial issues of its own and had held the finals just sixteen years before. It soon emerged that the president of Mexican TV network Televisa was a friend of Havelange's; 'My conscience is clear,' said the Brazilian, but no-one believed him.

Argy-bargy

Of all the World Cup machinations, the conspiracy that arguably holds the most weight is the involvement of Argentina's brutal military junta in the outcome of the 1978 tournament. General Jorge Rafael Videla ruled over the country with an iron fist, and stories emerged, even as the tournament was still being played, of referees being paid and military thugs threatening players from both the host nation and opposition. The most blatant example of Videla's influence came in the infamous second-round group game between Argentina and Peru, an eyebrow-raising 6–0 result that was contended to be a fix in a 1986 exposé in *The Sunday Times* (see Chapter 8 for more details).

Although the fix, and the junta's involvement, has never been proven definitively, an interesting footnote to the tournament took place in 2003, when a French radio host took a call from a man claiming to be an ex-international with insider knowledge of doping at the 1978 finals. The caller — who disguised his voice with an awful René from *'Allo 'Allo!* French accent (or maybe that was just how he spoke) — claimed several Argentina players took pills before their controversial game against *Les Bleus* and said it was obvious they were high on amphetamines both during and after the game. The whistleblower also said FIFA officials paid off a drug tester to 'forget' to test the Argentina players after the game. Naturally, Argentina denies any of this took place.

Ronaldo is dead!

One of the strangest modern-day conspiracies took place during the build-up to the 1998 World Cup Final between France and Brazil. The first signs of unrest were noted when the *Seleçao* failed to take the field for their customary pre-game warm-ups. When the media received the official team sheet with talismanic striker Ronaldo's name not included in Brazil's starting XI, the omission spread like wildfire through the press box, filtering out to the general populace too, before a FIFA official hastily gathered up the sheets and handed the media a new team sheet with Ronaldo reinstated to the starting line-up. The official blamed a communication error, but no-one was buying it, especially after Ronaldo ran around in a daze for ninety minutes.

Stories emerged that the Brazil striker had some kind of convulsion or fit in his hotel before the match; teammate Roberto Carlos was said to be heard screaming 'Ronaldo is dead!' as he ran down the corridor for help. The cause of the 'fit' was a source of much rumour and innuendo, ranging from a 'nervous crisis', a reaction to a painkilling injection in his knee, or a breakdown due to his girlfriend at the time having an affair with a journalist, depending on whose whispers you believed. Furthermore, stories emerged of a conspiracy by the Brazilian Football Federation and kit sponsors Nike to ensure the country's poster boy was on the field no matter what — although a Brazilian parliamentary enquiry in 2000 found no evidence of interference from the sportswear giant.

Cospirazione!

Over the years Brazil have been involved in their fair share of controversy, but where would the World Cup be without the conspiracy-crazy Italians to lend a little bit of legitimacy to proceedings? In 2002 the Italian press shouted *'Cospirazione!'* after they were knocked out in the Round of 16 by South Korea thanks to a last-minute strike by Ahn Jung-Hwan. *La Gazzetta dello Sport* said: 'We were knocked out in order to level out some old problems between us and the bosses of FIFA and UEFA. Shame on them, shame on the World Cup.'

Ecuadorian referee Byron Moreno, who sent off Francesco Totti for diving and disallowed a perfectly good goal, was pilloried in Italy (they made up a story that he was bought a new car after the tournament) and, for once, the accusations might have been on the right track. While nothing untoward was ever proven in the South Korea vs. Italy game, Moreno was later arrested for heroin trafficking in the USA and was sentenced to two years in jail — hardly a ringing endorsement to his integrity.

Brazil nuts

With the interpipe and Twitter offering a perfect soapbox, football has been fertile ground for conspiracy theories in the 21st century. While most are just hot air, one theory that gained enough traction to be reported by Eurosport and Slate.com was that the 2014 World Cup draw was rigged.

The first sign that something was awry came from a Spanish language Twitter account – @FraudeMundial14 – that correctly predicted the teams selected in Group F (Argentina, Nigeria, Iran and Bosnia and Herzegovina) a day *before* the 6 December draw. One tweet stated: 'It isn't our intention to destroy all expectations of the cup draw. That's why we only publish the group in which Argentina will participate.'

Then came a YouTube video (again in Spanish) that highlighted the differing ways FIFA secretary general Jerome Valcke and Brazilian actress Fernanda Lima drew the team names out of the sealed balls they were handed during the official draw. After opening a ball and taking out the slip of paper, Valcke moves his hands downwards and out of sight for a couple of seconds before raising them again to show the team name; Lima opens her balls and takes the paper out in plain view. The video suggests Valcke has ample time to replace the original piece of paper with a team name of FIFA's choosing placed out of sight of the cameras. (To back up this notion, another eagle-eyed conspiracy theorist noted Lima's pieces of paper curled back up when she put them down, as you might expect of a piece of paper that was rolled up inside a ball; Valcke's papers were flatter and stiffer.)

Valcke's sleight of hand was said to be a way in which FIFA could manipulate the groups to their liking, punishing teams they had gripes with (USA, Australia and England) and paving the way for a marquee Brazil–Argentina final (both South American sides were given easy groups). But then FIFA would never do something so corrupt, would they …?

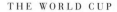

– 10 –

THE WEIRD AND
WONDERFUL WORLD CUP

Although very few of the strange, extraordinary and quite frankly scarcely believable tales documented in this chapter would ever make it into an official history of the tournament, they are the very bedrock of the World Cup's enduring mystique.

Of course, times, dates, results and scorers are all essential to building a record of events, but without these little moments of indiscretion, vexation, irrationality, joyfulness and heartbreak, the World Cup's history would be incomplete.

And let's face it — what would the tournament be without the accounts of a dog peeing on an England striker in the middle of a game, a Dutchman predicting his World Cup goal (but not foreseeing his sending-off), a grumpy coach telling his staff not to celebrate after just winning the World Cup, and an Argentinean exacting revenge on his country's dictator by shaking his hand seconds after soaping up his sweaty meat and two veg?

Let the madness begin.

Controversial beginnings

It took all of two days for the first World Cup to erupt into controversy. France took on Argentina in Montevideo on 15 July 1930, and a highly partisan Uruguayan crowd were already unhappy about their River Plate rivals being a goal up. They felt Luis Monti's free-kick goal had been taken too hastily, but France were coming on strong in the final ten minutes and an equalising goal seemed inevitable. That was, until Brazilian referee Gilberto de Almeida

THE WEIRD AND WONDERFUL WORLD CUP

Rêgo blew up for full-time a full six minutes early, just as France winger Marcel Langiller was flying down the wing towards goal.

Unsurprisingly, it all kicked off. The France players surrounded the ref, closely followed by their coach, Raoul Caudron. Then the Uruguayan fans invaded the pitch, becoming involved in some calm and measured lobbying on behalf of France, before the mounted police took to the field to restore order. After much gesticulating and shouting of swear words in at least three languages, Rêgo copped to his 'mistake' and asked the teams to play the final minutes. This proved easier said than done, however, as several Argentina players had broken down in tears celebrating their first victory, and inside-left Roberto Cerro had fainted with excitement. When the match was finally restarted, France couldn't regain their earlier momentum to level the scores and the World Cup had its first — but by no means last — controversial incident.

Down by law

Argentina striker Guillermo Stábile scored a tournament-best eight goals in 1930, but the man known as '*El Filtrador*' only got his chance to play in the first team due to a teammate's dedication to his studies. Manuel Ferreira made the decision to miss Argentina's second group game against Mexico so he could pop back over the River Plate to take a law exam. Stábile took his place and promptly scored a hat-trick against Mexico, two against the USA in the semi and another in the final. Stábile returned home a national hero, while the unlucky Ferreira was said to have drowned his sorrows at the bar. (The bar — he's trying to be a lawyer, geddit?)

The long leg of the law

The home team are always said to have an advantage, but Uruguay were given a helping hand, or foot, from an unlikely source in their 1930 semifinal against Yugoslavia. With Uruguay making a foray forward, the ball appeared to go out for a Yugoslavia throw-in, only for a policeman on the touchline to kick the ball back into play towards one of his compatriots. It proved to be a killer ball, as *La Celeste* scored their second directly from the policeman's pass and ran out 6–1 winners on the way to winning the first World Cup trophy.

It's a knockout

In 1930's other semifinal, between the USA and Argentina, the USA's trainer Jack Coll ran onto the pitch to attend to a stricken player only to be led off in a state of semi-consciousness just seconds later. It seems he slipped on the pitch and inhaled the contents of a bottle of chloroform that had broken in his bag. He had to do the woozy walk of shame back to the dugout in the arms of some giggling colleagues.

These aren't the finals you're looking for

There are many routes to ensuring qualification to the World Cup finals, but possibly the most assured is to ask your opponents not to play against you. In 1934, Italy were required to play a qualifier to book their place in the finals — the only host nation to ever do so — and came up with an ingenious way to make sure they progressed. After a 4–0 first-leg win against Greece in Milan, they managed to talk their opponents into not bothering to play the second leg. Of course, an Italian-funded property built for the Greek FA in Athens had nothing to do with the decision ...

The earliest of early exits

There are early exits and then there is Mexico in 1934. Having already qualified for the tournament, Mexico had only just touched down in Italy when they were told they had to play another 'qualifier' after the USA submitted a late application to take part — so late that the groups had already been decided.

Rather than telling the USA to bugger off — or building their FA a new building in New York — Mexico agreed to the game, and duly lost 4–2. They were knocked out of the World Cup before it had started, and they couldn't even cash in on their 20,000 kilometres of air miles as they hadn't been invented yet.

The longest game ev … zzzzzzzzz

Interminably dull games often seem to last longer than ninety minutes, but none have lasted as long as the 1934 quarterfinal between Italy and Spain. The first match in Florence ended 1–1, and when extra time still couldn't separate the two (there were no penalty shootouts back then), FIFA bigwigs had to act fast to find a winner. With the spectre of Mussolini lurking everywhere in '34, the chance of Italy being sent home on a coin toss was not worth contemplating, so the first replay in World Cup history was hurriedly agreed upon for the next day. Both teams were forced to make several changes, but Italy proved stronger as a first-half header from Inter Milan striker Giuseppe Meazza proved the difference — a full twenty-four hours after the game first kicked off.

'Bet you can't do that again'

When most players score with an outrageous piece of luck, they keep their mouth shut and let the air of mystery surrounding the goal imply a) they meant to do it and b) they could do it again whenever they want, when it is clear neither is the case. Shame Italy striker Raimundo Orsi couldn't keep his trap shut after scoring a stunning goal in the 1934 World Cup Final.

His stupendous curling strike with the outside of his right boot fooled the Czechoslovakia keeper to send the match into extra time and, after Italy won the game 2–1, rather than admitting it was a fluke, he said he could do it again on demand. The next day, in front of the world's press, he made twenty attempts to replicate the goal. He missed all twenty.

Don't look under the bed

Shoeboxes kept underneath beds typically contain things people don't want to keep: old pens that don't work, faded pictures of a girl you snogged on holiday as a teenager, a video cassette with old recordings of *Alf* (but, strangely enough, never shoes). So maybe there was some logic in Italian FA chief Ottorino Barassi keeping the World Cup trophy stuffed under his mattress in an old shoebox during the war years. It proved an effective hiding place from those trophy-melting fascists who roamed Europe in the '40s, and Barassi's hiding place kept it safe so it could go on to be stolen another two times before finally disappearing for good.

Thanks for coming

The Dutch East Indies have the unenviable record of being the only country to have played just one game at the World Cup. They lost 6–0 to Hungary in 1938 and, due to the tournament's knockout system, they had to return home after only ninety minutes of football. As the minimum number of World Cup games is now three and the Dutch East Indies no longer exists (for those who haven't been to school since the 1940s, it is now Indonesia), it's also a record that will never be broken.

'But I thought we were a shoe-in'

Nations have pulled out of the finals for many different reasons — travel distances, politics, sulking because they weren't asked to be hosts — but none had a better excuse than India in 1950: they didn't want to wear boots. The barefoot India had performed admirably in the 1948 Olympics, only losing 2–1 to France, but FIFA informed India of their 'compulsory footwear' rule at the eleventh hour and they were forced to pull out of the tournament, despite being allocated a group to play in. Legend has it that after India froze their bollo … sorry, toes off in the 1952 Helsinki Olympics they decided to put some boots on after all.

Girder of God

The 1950 group game between Brazil and Yugoslavia pitted two of the tournament favourites against each other, and 142,429 fans packed into the Maracanã to witness it. As if a partisan crowd wasn't enough to put Yugoslavia at a disadvantage, they had to start the match with just ten men after Rajko Mitić injured his bonce walking out of the dressing rooms; he smacked his head on a girder that was sticking out in a part of the stadium where construction had yet to be finished. Brazil were already a goal up when the bandaged defender finally returned to the pitch, and the home team ran out 2–0 winners.

'Don't blame it on the sunshine …'

The 1954 quarterfinal between Austria and Switzerland was one of the most exciting games in the history of the tournament. After twenty-three minutes the Switzerland were 3–0 up, only for Austria to score five goals in nine minutes against a famed defensive system that was known as the *verrou*, or 'door bolt'.

Having had their door so comprehensively kicked in, Switzerland pulled one back to make it a respectable 5–4 at the half. An account written by a Swiss journalist, handed out in the press box at the other match taking place at the time, tried to place the blame elsewhere: 'All goals scored against Switzerland owing to the sun.' Only three goals were scored in a 'boring' second half, with Austria winning 7–5 in the highest-scoring game in World Cup history.

It's gotta be the shoes

Germany captain Fritz Walter was well known for playing better as the weather conditions worsened, due to the malaria he'd contracted during the war playing havoc with his constitution in the heat. So when it began pelting with rain on the day of the final in 1954, Germany thought they might be in with a chance against the all-conquering Hungary. What they didn't tell anyone else was that they had a secret weapon for the match — newfangled 'screw-in' studs on their new adidas boots were designed to give them more traction in muddy conditions. While the Magical Magyars found it hard to find their feet in the final, Germany marched to victory 3–2.

Trophy trailblazer

Although it is difficult to verify, the story goes that Brazil captain Bellini was the first person to lift the World Cup trophy above his head in celebration, in what is now a go-to move of captains around the world. Many of the photographers missed the official presentation of the trophy after the 1958 final, so they asked Bellini to re-create the moment on the pitch, and he hoisted the trophy in the air so everyone could get a good photo.

It's a dog's life

The 1962 quarterfinal in Viña del Mar between Brazil and England saw one of the most mesmerising and elusive performances in the history of the tournament. However, it didn't come from one of the Brazilian samba boys or an English lion, but from a Chilean dog that had run onto the pitch. The pooch had a sniff around the England box before heading off on a mazy run through the middle of the park, and it's here legendary English commentator Kenneth Wolstenholme should take over:

> 66 Now Garrincha is going to have a shot
> [at catching the dog]. This is Garrincha, No. 7 …
> [the dog has] a better body swerve than Garrincha's
> got. Now Jimmy Greaves … Will he …?
> … Well done, Jimmy! Jimmy Greaves, already
> the hero of this game but the dog obviously
> [doesn't] like being sent off so early … 99

Greavsie was seen wringing his hands as he escorted the dog from the pitch and he later revealed the canine had lost control of its bladder in all the fun and games.

'I smelt so bad it was awful,' said Greaves later. 'I should have won the game for England, because no Brazilian defenders came near me.'

'The Little Bird' off the hook

When Brazil forward — and the 1962 final's undoubted star — Garrincha was given a red card for a seemingly innocuous foul on Chile's Eladio Rojas in the semifinal, it meant that he would be suspended for the final against Czechoslovakia. The Brazilian merely tapped the Chilean on his behind, but Rojas went down like a sack of spuds and the linesman informed the ref that it was a red card offence.

FIFA had already set a precedent by banning other players given their marching orders, but the 'The Little Bird' had some powerful friends, including the president of Peru, who asked the Peruvian ref to let Garrincha off the hook. With the linesman who witnessed the incident not able to provide testimony — he disappeared to Paris on a ticket paid for by a Brazilian FIFA representative — the case against Garrincha collapsed and he was allowed to play in the final, where he helped Brazil to a 3–1 win over Czechoslovakia.

Swingin' sixties

With more instances of brazen thuggery and violence than a Saturday night in Kings Cross, the 1966 tournament should have come with an 'R' rating. It all ... erm, kicked off with a vicious tackle by England enforcer Nobby Stiles on Frenchman Jacques Simon (which led to rumours of FIFA requesting Stiles be dropped from Alf Ramsey's team). Then, Argentina were issued with an official warning for their tasty tackling against West Germany. Brazil were given a torrid time throughout the tournament, with both Garrincha and Pelé kicked from pillar to (goal)post, the latter being literally kicked out of the tournament by Portugal and left contemplating retirement.

But it all came to the boil in two of the quarterfinals. Argentina's dirty tricks against England led to coach Alf Ramsey calling their players 'animals' and, in the game between Uruguay and Germany, Horacio Troche responded to a foul from Lothar Emmerich by aiming a kick to his stomach. As he jogged off the pitch after being given a red card, he slapped Uwe Seeler in the face for good measure. Two for one!

No celebrations, please, we're British

When Geoff Hurst scored England's decisive fourth goal — and the third of a historic hat-trick — in the 1966 final against West Germany at Wembley, the home bench exploded into celebration. Except for head coach and serial grump Alf Ramsey, that is. The England manager remained statue-like on the bench, even shouting at trainer Harold Shepherdson to 'sit down and behave yourself, man'.

THE WEIRD AND WONDERFUL WORLD CUP

Moore is innocent

If ever a list was compiled of World Cup participants likely to steal stuff, Bobby Moore wouldn't be on it. England's Captain Fantastic was a beacon of fair play and honesty, so when the West Ham defender was accused by a sales assistant of stealing a gold necklace in a Bogotá hotel ahead of the 1970 finals, most people smelled a rat. Everyone except the Colombian authorities, that is, who arrested Moore for allegedly pocketing an emerald and diamond necklace worth £600, causing him to miss the team's flight to Mexico and putting his tournament in jeopardy.

With England's leader sitting in a jail cell, a diplomatic incident was brewing, especially as Prime Minister Harold Wilson became involved in negotiations. When a reconstruction of events proved that Moore could not have stolen the necklace (the sales assistant said the necklace was put in Moore's left pocket, but his trousers didn't have a pocket on that side), the 'theft' was exposed as a scam and the nation's captain was released five days before England's first game. Although clearly a racket, charges were not dropped for another two years. Moore was finally sent a 'letter of pardon' in December 1975.

You'll never win anything with kids

If you've ever seen a schoolboy game of football where the kids run riot and the referee loses all control of the game, then you'll have sympathy for referee Ali Kandil during the Mexico vs. El Salvador group game in 1970. Not that the Egyptian was completely blameless in turning two teams of grown men into petulant schoolkids. It started with Kandil giving a vague refereeing decision of some kind to one of the two teams playing, although neither team knew whom it was for. El Salvador believed it was for a foul in their favour, but a Mexico player took a quick free kick the other way and *El Tri* scored from the resulting move.

Understandably, El Salvador were a bit miffed and surrounded the ref at the centre spot. They clearly didn't want to restart the game so, after having to run to the goal to retrieve the ball himself, the ref placed it on the centre circle, only for a player to kick it off the spot like a sulky five-year-old. This 'player kicking the ball, ref re-placing the ball on the spot' shenanigans continued for a good couple of minutes until the ref finally decided to book someone, at which point all the El Salvador players turned their back to the ref, imploring him to book the entire team, 'I am Spartacus'–style. In the end, clearly realising that he was dealing with the footballing equivalent of a kindergarten class, the ref gave up and blew for half-time. Bloody kids.

Playing football *is* rocket science

It's a little-known fact that Brazil's victory in the 1970 World Cup was heavily influenced by the space race between the USA and Russia at the time. How? With vast sums of money being invested in sending man into space, the world's best and brightest were invited to NASA to lend their expertise, including Brazil's fitness coach Cláudio Coutinho, who was a retired army captain and military physical training expert. He studied some of the training exercises used to get astronauts prepared for the Apollo missions and returned to South America with a fitness regime never seen before in football.

Brazil's training camp in Guanajuato in May was run like a military boot camp, but it paid dividends as the *Seleçao* were by far the fittest team in the tournament. Which just goes to show what running around playing two hours of football in a full astronaut suit will do for a player's stamina.

Giving England the finger

England manager Alf Ramsey was a bit of a Little Englander, always railing against foreign players and that horrible foreign muck they had to eat on away trips. So it surprised few when the 1970 England team organised to bring their own food with them to Mexico to avoid being struck down by Montezuma's revenge. The move angered their Mexican hosts, prompting one newspaper to write: 'If you are going to throw fruit at the England team, remember to wash it first.' Much of the imported English food was burnt by officials when it arrived at the dock (as in destroyed, not badly cooked) and the players were forced to live on a diet of fish fingers, which was strangely allowed through customs as an 'acceptable food stuff'. Yum.

'The Save'

The 1970 group game between England and Brazil witnessed what is now known simply as 'The Save'. England keeper Gordon Banks threw himself down to parry Pelé's goal-bound header up and over the bar in a feat of agility and dexterity of the highest order. The Brazilian later said of the moment:

> **At that moment I hated Gordon Banks more than any man in soccer. But when I cooled down I had to applaud him with my heart for the greatest save I have ever seen.**

Australia causes yellow fever

There must be something about Australian group-stage matches in Germany that make referees temporarily lose all ability to count. The Socceroos made their first appearance in the finals in 1974 and, in their game against Chile, midfielder Ray Richards was given a yellow card in both halves by Iranian ref Jafar Namdar —

but wasn't given his marching orders. He was allowed to play on for another five minutes before reserve official Clive Thomas had a word with the linesman about Namdar's lack of mathematical prowess and Richards was sent for an early shower.

Thirty-two years later in the do-or-die match between Australia and Croatia, English ref Graham Poll only sent off Croatian defender Josip Šimunić after giving him three yellows (on sixty-one, ninety and ninety-three minutes). Poll's excuse was that he had mistakenly written Šimunić down as the Australian No.3 for the first booking — an easy mistake, considering Šimunic grew up in Australia and speaks English with an Aussie accent. An 'easy mistake', other than the fact he was wearing the red-and-white pizza restaurant–tablecloth Croatia kit …

One-touch football

Many keepers like to have an early touch of the ball so they can calm their nerves and get into the flow of the game. Germany goalkeeper Sepp Maier got his gloves on the ball with less than two minutes gone in the 1974 World Cup Final, but not in the calming way he would've hoped. The Teutonic custodian's first touch was picking the ball out of the back of the net after the Netherlands' Johan Neeskens had smashed a penalty (the quickest World Cup Final goal in history) past him. In fact, the Netherlands got off to such a devastating start — Cruyff taking off on a mazy run through the heart of the opposition's defence before being cut down in the box — that Maier was the first Germany player to touch the ball, period.

More than a game

A hero to the Dutch nation when he helped unleash Total Football on the Netherlands' unsuspecting opponents during the 1974 World Cup, Johan Cruyff was public enemy number one four years later, as his refusal to play in the 1978 tournament was seen as the reason the *Oranje* lost a second consecutive final.

His motive for not travelling to Argentina were unclear, but there were rumours his sponsorship deal with Puma had led to a falling-out with the adidas-loving Dutch federation, or he objected to host nation's military junta. In fact, the reason remained a secret for thirty years, until Cruyff admitted during a radio interview in 2008 that a failed kidnap attempt on his family a few months before the tournament led to him staying at home.

Living in Barcelona at the time, Cruyff and his wife were tied up in front of their children and the would-be kidnappers pointed a gun at his head before he managed to escape and raise the alarm. The next few weeks were a blur of security guards and armed escorts, and the increased scrutiny — from money-seeking kidnappers to story-hungry press — led to a changed outlook on life.

'All these things change your point of view towards many things,' said Cruyff on Catalunya Radio. 'There are moments in life in which there are other values ... It was the moment to leave football and I couldn't play in the World Cup after this.'

Having a laugh

Dutchman Dick Nanninga only played fifteen games for the Netherlands, but he carved out his place in World Cup folklore thanks to two curious incidents in the 1978 finals. Firstly, he predicted that he would come on in the final as a substitute and score a goal with ten minutes left, even boasting to the world's media this would happen in the days leading up to the match.

However, his guess was off the mark — he actually scored with nine minutes to go, heading the ball past Ubaldo Fillol in the 81st minute of the final. Unfortunately his fortune-telling skills didn't help him earlier in the tournament, as he failed to foresee that laughing at the referee's decision to yellow card him in the match against West Germany would lead to a red card and a place in history as the first substitute to be sent off in the World Cup.

Argentinean ball juggling

Although they played with pride for their country, many of the Argentina players were privately opposed to General Videla's leadership during the 1978 World Cup. Some were directly affected by his brutal policies, including defender Alberto Tarantini, who had many friends who were 'disappeared'.

Just before Videla entered the changing room to congratulate the team on winning the World Cup, Tarantini, looking for revenge, bet captain Daniel Passarella $1000 that he would shake the general's hand after soaping up his balls (the pink dangly ones, not the adidas Tango). The wager was agreed upon, a soapy hand was extended, and Tarantini was a grand better off.

'I'll never forget his expression afterwards,' said Tarantini of the general. 'He just glared at me. But I don't regret what I did.'

A bit of a sheik-up

Kuwait players were onto a winner when they qualified for the 1982 finals in Spain, with each member of the twenty-four-man squad being given a Cadillac, a luxury villa, a plot of land and a speedboat by their wealthy backers. But the problem with being supported by wealthy sheiks is that they don't particularly like it when things don't go their way — or at least that was the case with Kuwait's Prince Fahad Al-Ahmed Al-Jaber Al-Sabah during his country's group game against France.

Already 3–1 up, France's Alain Giresse scored what looked to be a fourth, but the Kuwait players complained that they had stopped after hearing a whistle. Referee Myroslav Stupar was having none of it and signalled a goal. In the stands, Fahad, president of the Kuwaiti FA and brother of the emir, stood up and gave a wave of his hand and the entire Kuwait team suddenly made their way from the field.

The prince took to the pitch, along with a bunch of Spanish soldiers, and after some tense negotiations the game restarted — but with Stupar now disallowing the goal and starting again with a drop-ball. Prince Fahad was fined a derisory £8000 for his part in the fuss (no gold leaf–infused toothpaste this week, Prince …) and Stupar never reffed a World Cup game again.

Never work with orphans or animals

As well as having several problems with infrastructure and organisation ahead of the 1982 finals, it seems Spain had a dearth of media-savvy orphans too. FIFA decided to invite a group of boys from a local Madrid orphanage to help out with the first-ever televised World Cup draw. In front of a packed audience and hundreds of millions of global viewers, the young lads had to remove plastic footballs from revolving cages and hand them to FIFA bigwigs as part of the draw ceremony.

Unfortunately, the boys weren't treating events with the gravity required (although they weren't aided by the faulty cages), resulting in teams being revealed ahead of time and two teams being placed in the wrong group. At one point a FIFA delegate could be heard on the live TV coverage shouting at one of the nervous lads: 'Get it sorted, boy!'

As well as the PR disaster — for both FIFA's organisational skills and the Spanish orphans' chances of ever being adopted — the late-running ceremony delayed the Spanish lottery for the first and only time in its history.

Ref off

France could rightly feel aggrieved about Dutch referee Charles Corver's shocking decision not to red card Harald Schumacher for his heinous foul on Patrick Battiston in the 1982 semifinal, but the French FA only have themselves to blame for Corver being the man in black.

In his great book *Twelve Yards: The Art and Psychology of the Perfect Penalty*, writer Ben Lyttleton discovered FFF delegate Roger Machin had vetoed Spanish ref José António Garrido's selection for the semi, believing the Spaniard's officiating of France's loss to England was a bad omen. Corver was drafted in as the replacement and although he awarded a penalty that Platini scored to bring the scores level at 1–1, his non-call early in the second half changed the course of the game. *Sacré bleu!*

'Aaaargggghhhhh!'

In the early summer of 1982 you might have been forgiven for thinking there was an epidemic of wasps descending on school playgrounds across Europe; young boys could be seen running around, shaking their heads from side to side and going apeshit, as if to escape a horde of giant stingers.

In fact they were just emulating one of the greatest goal celebrations in World Cup history: Marco Tardelli's after scoring Italy's second goal in the 1982 World Cup Final. His euphoric 'arms out, head shaking in disbelief' exaltation is an iconic image in Italian football history and became known as the 'Tardelli Scream'.

'In sport or in life, nothing compares to that moment,' Tardelli said of his wonder strike.

Wave for the camera

The opening match of the 1986 World Cup finals between Mexico and Belgium was said to be the first time *La Ola* — known more popularly as 'The Mexican Wave' — was performed at a football match, although other sports have been quick to insist they were the originators. American cheerleader George Henderson claimed he invented it, saying he started it off at hockey games in the '70s; another American said that he began a 'wave' at a college football game, while other observers recalled seeing it in 1970 when the finals were also in Mexico.

Just who came up with the concept will never be proven, but looking at how waves are usually originated — by bored people with limited attention spans and no real interest in the subtleties of the game in front of them — it does seem more than likely to be an American invention ...

Stop celebrating, lads. We've got a game in four years

Argentina boss Carlos Bilardo clearly came from the Alf Ramsey school of celebrating a World Cup win (see 'No celebrations, please, we're British'). After his team triumphed in a thrilling World Cup Final in 1986, he heard his players celebrating raucously in the showers and went in to have a word.

'We were in the shower singing,' said defender José Luis Brown, who scored the opening goal.

> And he told us, 'Just remember we've got a World Cup to defend in 1990.' Only a half an hour earlier we had won the World Cup, and he was already thinking of the next one.

The curse of the keeper

One of the curses of being a goalkeeper is that, no matter how well you play, a moment of blinding skill (or luck) can undo all your hard work in a second. Two examples of the 'keeper's curse' are Belgium's Michel Preud'homme and England's Peter Shilton, both considered as one of their country's all-time greats but also forever linked to letting in two of the greatest goals in tournament history.

In Preud'homme's case, he was voted top goalkeeper of the 1994 tournament but was powerless to stop a brilliant solo effort from Saudi Arabia's Saeed Al-Owairan, who started deep from inside his own area and slipped past the Belgium defenders like a mussel sliding out of its shell. Shilton, who once held the record for the most minutes without conceding a goal in the finals, was unlucky enough to be between the sticks in 1986 when Diego Maradona decided to give the World Cup the gift of the greatest goal ever scored. (Shilts is just as famous for being the man who couldn't out-jump a midget for El Diego's first 'Hand of God' goal.)

Who'd be a keeper, eh?

'Hey, over here! It's me, the World Cup finals!'

The USA has been notoriously slow to take football under its sporting wing, with much of the apathy owing to an already crowded and competitive sporting landscape. But nothing could have prepared the organisers of USA 94 for what the World Cup opening ceremony on 17 June 1994 had to compete with on the American airwaves.

In New York, ice hockey's New York Rangers were celebrating their Stanley Cup championship with a parade through the streets of Manhattan and the city's Knicks were playing the Houston Rockets in the NBA Finals — while in Oakmont, Pennsylvania, golfing legend Arnold Palmer was bidding farewell to the public in his final round in the US Open.

If that wasn't enough to draw fans away from the world's biggest sporting event, it was also the day former American football star OJ Simpson led police on a chase along a Los Angeles freeway in his white Ford Bronco. Events from that not-so-high-speed chase were famously beamed live on every US network, leaving thousands of Bolivia and Germany fans who thought it would be a good idea to watch the opening game at the pub both angry and disappointed.

A win dedicated to the treacherous bastards

When Brazil captain Dunga raised the World Cup trophy above his head in the Pasadena Rose Bowl on 16 July 1994, he didn't shout a 'Get in there!', 'You beauty!' or any other Brazilian exclamation of joy. He actually went on a potty-mouthed tirade at the media, who had doubted and criticised the *Seleçao* for their dour footballing style during the tournament.

My Brazilian isn't the best, but it went something along the lines of this:

> ❝This is for you, you treacherous bastards! What do you say now? Come on, take the pictures, you bunch of treacherous motherfuckers! It's for you!❞

Charming.

Bin Laden's deadly World Cup plot

Three years before the shocking terrorist strike on the Twin Towers in New York City, Osama bin Laden had planned to use the 1998 World Cup in France to launch a devastating attack on the England and US national teams. The plot involved killing the England team with chemical weapons while they were on the pitch at the Stade Vélodrome in Marseille for their opening game against Tunisia, while another group of terrorists was to storm the US team's hotel and kill the players as they watched the game on TV. The plot was only uncovered two weeks before the match from intelligence gathered from suspects arrested in Belgium.

Not much was made of the plot being foiled at the time, so as not to heighten fears, but the legacy of the plot — and the events of 9/11 — led to extreme measures being deployed in the 2002 finals in Korea and Japan. UK paper *The Daily Mail* reported that anti-aircraft missiles had been set up inside the World Cup Stadium in Seoul for the opening game between

France and Senegal, and patrolling helicopters, submarines and warships were on high alert. All flights within six miles of the stadium were also diverted two hours before and after the game.

Blond ambition

After securing their passage into the knockout phase of the 1998 tournament with a last-minute 2–1 win over England in Toulouse, the Romanian team decided to celebrate with a bit of team bonding in the communal bathrooms.

When they emerged for their final group game against Tunisia, every player had dyed their hair blond (except for keeper Bogdan Stelea, who had a lack of hair to dye in the first place). Coach Anghel Iordănescu, who shaved his head instead of dyeing it, said: 'This is a bonding exercise and lucky charm to carry us all the way to the final.'

To the relief of sore-eyed commentators the world over, Romania were promptly knocked out in the Round of 16 by the sensible short back and side–sporting Croatia.

Name that tune

During the 1998 finals, bored England players decided to have a bet to see how many song names they could mention in on-air interviews with the BBC and ITV. It didn't take long for the wager to take effect: defender Tony Adams managed to get three in the first sentence of one interview with Des Lynam: 'I'm so excited, we've had some magic moments this season and it just gets better and better …'; fellow defender Gareth Southgate answered a Bob Wilson question with, 'It's hardly Club Tropicana, Bob, it's been raining all day … you're not going to get any careless whispers from me … about the team'; while captain Alan Shearer deadpanned: 'We're all excited but we weren't exactly dancing on the ceiling.'

This speaking in clichés was supposed to be easily noticeable for the watching football fans, but this is England footballers we're talking about here; for serial dullard Shearer, they were some of the best interviews he had ever given. In the end, journalist Ray Stubbs got wind of the antics and asked the England captain about the bet: 'It's just your imagination, Ray,' said Shearer, before cracking up into his first laugh/smile combo ever seen in public.

A presidential decree

After scoring the final goal en route to winning the World Cup in 1998, France's Emmanuel Petit was celebrating in the locker room when French president Jacques Chirac approached him. The French leader congratulated the pony-tailed midfielder on his team's victory and then revealed a very sensitive piece of information.

Said Petit: 'The president came up to me, we shook hands and he looked at me and said, "You are the one my wife prefers."'

Ronaldo's a cut above

As well as being the World Cup's all-time leading goalscorer, Brazil's Ronaldo can also lay claim to having the worst haircut to ever grace the finals. Looking like a 'Brazilian gone wrong', his 'tuft at the front, bald at the back' was truly awful — but the alleged story behind the cut is cute enough for us to forgive him.

'Why did I have my crazy haircut?' said Ronnie.

❝I called home and [my wife] Milene said our son Ronald had rushed to the TV and kissed it, shouting, 'It's Daddy, Daddy.' But it wasn't me. It was Roberto Carlos. Can you imagine? He is so ugly. I said that cannot happen again. I must do something to make it impossible.❞

Smell you later!

David Beckham mania had already hit stratospheric heights by the time the 2002 World Cup finals kicked off in South Korea and Japan. His every move — especially a new 'Hoxton fin' Mohawk haircut — was analysed and commented on by the world's media.

But it wasn't just the fans who were besotted with the England midfielder — it seemed even Brazil striker Ronaldo had a crush on the squeaky-voiced underwear model after swapping shirts with him: 'Normally when you swap shirts with someone they are soaked in sweat, but Beckham's smelt of perfume. Either he protects himself against BO or he sweats cologne.' For a man known as 'Goldenballs', it's probably the latter …

Rivaldo goes down

Rivaldo was considered one of the best players in the world at the turn of the 21st century and he was critical to the success of Brazil in 2002, scoring goals and teeing up Ronaldo to fire the *Seleçao* to victory.

However, he will be forever remembered by some for one of the most cynical acts of play-acting ever seen in the tournament. When Turkey defender Hakan Ünsal kicked the ball at the Brazilian in frustration near the end of their first group game, hitting his thigh, Rivaldo went to the ground clutching his face, adding a few dramatic rolls for good measure.

The referee clearly only saw the reaction — what the assistant ref was looking at only a couple of feet away, we'll never know — and sent Unsal off. It was scant consolation for Turkey that after FIFA reviewed the incident Rivaldo was fined 11,500 Swiss francs for his antics.

No goals, no glory

Switzerland hold the unfortunate distinction of being the only team in the history of the World Cup to be knocked out despite not conceding a goal. In 2006, a 0–0 draw with France followed by 2–0 victories over Togo and South Korea saw the Swiss advance to a Round of 16 clash with Ukraine.

The two teams played out a 0–0 stalemate that went to a penalty shootout, which Switzerland lost 3–0. The Swiss played a total of 390 minutes without conceding and were still on the plane home. Coach Köbi Kuhn tried to remain philosophical: 'The recognition from our fans is the most positive thing. Let's forget the penalties and remember the clean sheets. We will keep on building.' The feat was even more amazing considering the Swiss played two and a half of those games with comedy defender Philippe Senderos as centre-half …

Worth the wait

Some fantastic goals have been scored in the history of the World Cup, but only one has been scored after the player's death. USA's Bert Patenaude had always asserted that he had completed the first hat-trick in the history of the tournament when he put three past Paraguay on 17 July 1930. Unfortunately, FIFA records only gave him two of the goals and Argentina's Guillermo Stábile was credited as the World Cup's first hat-trick hero for his trio of strikes two days later against Mexico.

When Patenaude was inducted into the US Soccer Hall of Fame in 1971, the question was raised again and the striker stuck to his guns that he had scored all three goals that day. It sparked some historically conscious researchers to action, who subsequently found match and newspaper reports and eyewitness accounts that backed up Bert's story. Patenaude passed away in 1974, and it took until November 2006 for FIFA officials to finally acknowledge the American as the man who had scored the World Cup's first hat-trick, the final goal coming thirty-two years after his death.

German joy, African heartbreak

Germany may have hosted one of the most well-organised finals in recent memory in 2006, but the way in which they were granted the hosting rights left much to be desired and shone a light on the shady dealings of FIFA. South Africa were favourites to host the 2006 tournament, especially after Sepp Blatter promised it to the African nations in return for voting him into the presidency ahead of France 98.

However, the European bloc was powerful and, after England were voted out, many delegates shifted their votes to Germany and the third and final ballot, held in Zurich in July 2000, was too close to call. With Germany leading 12–11, the final vote was held by seventy-eight-year-old New Zealand FIFA delegate Charles Dempsey, who defied the Oceania Confederation's wish that he vote for South Africa and abstained, handing the finals to Germany. Dempsey was vilified for his decision in both Africa and New Zealand, but he countered that he had been put under enormous pressure to vote a certain way: 'The pressure I was under was unsustainable,' said Dempsey.

> It was like a Hollywood production. On the last evening before the vote, my life became unbearable. I voted as I did because of the pressures put on me by various people.

Much of the pressure was said to have come from Blatter himself, wary of his promise to Africa but aware that Dempsey wanted to vote for Europe; the FIFA president even flew out to the Oceania Convention two months before the vote to persuade members to take a vote to urge Dempsey to vote for South Africa.

While Dempsey's legacy was forever tarnished, the 'Teflon don' Blatter came out of the debacle pretty well, not even losing African support despite his broken promise.

'He did the best he could for us; I don't think we could desert him now,' said one member of the South African bid committee about Blatter at the time.

Kim possible

After North Korea unsurprisingly failed to get out of their 2010 World Cup group (in that year's 'Group of Death' with Brazil, Portugal and Ivory Coast), the returning players and coaches were given a public dressing down by officials for 'betraying' leader Kim Jong-il and his country's ideals.

Held in an auditorium in the working people's culture palace in Pyongyang, the six-hour critical assault was led by Ri Dong-Kyu, an appropriately named sports commentator who laid into each individual player's performance in front of 400 athletes and sports students. There was even talk that coach Kim Jong-Hun and his charges had been sentenced to hard labour upon their return to the North.

Then there was the mystery of who the 1000 or so 'fans' seen cheering on North Korea during their matches were. There were rumours that they were paid Chinese actors (two Chinese PR firms confirmed they were recruited to find singers and dancers to attend the games), or ethnic North Koreans living in Japan. One fan, Kim Jong-chul, went on record as saying they were all military men handpicked by the regime to cheer for the side.

'The World Cup is nothing without me'

Footballers with big egos are nothing new, and Sweden's hugely talented but controversial striker Zlatan Ibrahimovic has never been shy about promoting his own talents. Among some of Ibra's best one-liners are his response to turning down a trial with Arsenal as a seventeen-year-old — 'Zlatan doesn't do auditions' — and his criticism of Barcelona coach Pep Guardiola's use of him during a disappointing two-year stint: 'You bought a Ferrari but you drive it like a Fiat.'

So it came as a surprise to a total of zero people that Ibrahimovic had a few things to say after Sweden were knocked out of the 2014 World Cup finals in a 4–2 playoff defeat to a Cristiano Ronaldo–inspired Portugal.

'One thing is for sure, a World Cup without me is nothing to watch, so it is not worthwhile to wait for the World Cup,' said Zlatan, displaying his usual humility.

Goodbye to an icon

The current World Cup trophy is due to be sent off to the big cabinet in the sky after the 2038 tournament, as there will be no more room on the base of the trophy for the winners' names. Thieves are said to be licking their lips at the chance of taking on the Brazilian FA's 'foolproof' security system again …

THE WORLD CUP
ROLL OF HONOUR

*A list of the notable winners from every World Cup
finals, from Uruguay 1930 to South Africa 2010.*

1930 Uruguay
Winner Uruguay
Runner-up Argentina
Third USA
Golden Boot (Most goals in the tournament)
Guillermo Stábile (Argentina) 8

1934 Italy
Winner Italy
Runner-up Czechoslovakia
Third Germany
Golden Boot Oldřich Nejedlý (Czechoslovakia) 5

1938 France
Winner Italy
Runner-up Hungary
Third Brazil
Golden Boot Leônidas (Brazil) 7

1950 Brazil
Winner Uruguay
Runner-up Brazil
Third Sweden
Golden Boot Ademir (Brazil) 7

1954 Switzerland
Winner West Germany
Runner-up Hungary
Third Austria
Golden Boot Sándor Kocsis (Hungary) 11

1958 Sweden
Winner Brazil
Runner-up Sweden
Third France
Golden Boot Just Fontaine (France) 13
Best Young Player Pelé (Brazil)

1962 Chile
Winner Brazil
Runner-up Czechoslovakia
Third Chile
Golden Boot Flórián Albert (Hungary), Garrincha
(Brazil), Valentin Ivanov (Russia), Drazen Jerkovic
(Yugoslavia), Leonel Sánchez (Chile), Vavá (Brazil) 4
Best Young Player Flórián Albert (Hungary)

1966 England
Winner England
Runner-up West Germany
Third Portugal
Golden Boot Eusébio (Portugal) 9
Best Young Player Franz Beckenbauer (West Germany)

1970 Mexico
Winner Brazil
Runner-up Italy
Third West Germany
Golden Boot Gerd Müller (West Germany) 10
Best Young Player Teófilo Cubillas (Peru)

1974 West Germany
Winner West Germany
Runner-up Netherlands
Third Poland
Golden Boot Grzegorz Lato (Poland) 7
Best Young Player Wladyslaw Zmuda (Poland)

1978 Argentina
Winner Argentina
Runner-up Netherlands
Third Brazil
Golden Boot Mario Kempes (Argentina) 6
Best Young Player Antonio Cabrini (Italy)

1982 Spain
Winner Italy
Runner-up West Germany
Third Poland
Golden Ball (Best Player) Paolo Rossi (Italy)
Golden Boot Paolo Rossi (Italy) 6
Best Young Player Manuel Amoros (France)

1986 Mexico
Winner Argentina
Runner-up West Germany
Third France
Golden Ball Diego Maradona (Argentina)
Golden Boot Gary Lineker (England) 6
Best Young Player Enzo Scifo (Belgium)

1990 Italy
Winner West Germany
Runner-up Argentina
Third Italy
Golden Ball Salvatore Schillaci (Italy)
Golden Boot Salvatore Schillaci (Italy) 6
Best Young Player Robert Prosinecki (Yugoslavia)

1994 USA
Winner Brazil
Runner-up Italy
Third Sweden
Golden Ball Romário (Brazil)
Golden Boot Oleg Salenko (Russia), Hristo Stoichkov (Bulgaria) 6
Best Young Player Marc Overmars (Netherlands)
Best Goalkeeper Michel Preud'homme (Belgium)

1998 France
Winner France
Runner-up Brazil
Third Croatia
Golden Ball Ronaldo (Brazil)
Golden Boot Davor Suker (Croatia) 6
Best Young Player Michael Owen (England)
Best Goalkeeper Fabien Barthez (France)

2002 Korea/Japan
Winner Brazil
Runner-up Germany
Third Turkey
Golden Ball Oliver Kahn (Germany)
Golden Boot Ronaldo (Brazil) 8
Best Young Player Landon Donovan (USA)
Best Goalkeeper Oliver Kahn (Germany)

2006 Germany
Winner Italy
Runner-up France
Third Germany
Golden Ball Zinedine Zidane (France)
Golden Boot Miroslav Klose (Germany) 5
Best Young Player Lukas Podolski (Germany)
Best Goalkeeper Gianluigi Buffon (Italy)

2010 South Africa
Winner Spain
Runner-up Netherlands
Third Germany
Golden Ball Diego Forlan (Uruguay)
Golden Boot Thomas Müller (Germany) 5
Best Young Player Thomas Müller (Germany)
Best Goalkeeper Iker Casillas (Spain)

ACKNOWLEDGEMENTS

Thanks to Line, Morten, Ulla and Henning for providing me with a great working environment to write the book and to Ben Lyttleton for being a great sounding board and an even better friend.

A big *danke/tak/gracias/grazie* to Frauke Powell, Halfdan Bock Andersen, Martin Mazur and Sara Tambini for the help with the difficult foreign words.

And for the difficult English words, a heartfelt thanks to my brilliant editor Allison Hiew.

Finally, to Karina, for running my tea to the office when I left it on the kitchen table. What would I do without you …? x